THE CHESAPEAKE

OYSTER BUYBOATS, SHIPS & STEAMED CRABS

KEN ROSSIGNOL
LARRY JARBOE

About the cover: The historic Chesapeake Bay Oyster Buyboat is shown returning to the Cape Charles, Virginia harbor with a large freighter in the distance, depicting two centuries of shipping on the Chesapeake. Photo by Ken Rossignol

Contents

Introduction

Welcome aboard the third volume of THE CHESAPEAKE – This book, THE CHESAPEAKE: Oyster Buyboats, Ships & Steamed Crabs, spans the decades of the lives of our writers and the times of the Chesapeake Tidewater region from 1900 to the present time.

A first-person account of Chesapeake Bay bounty being harvested and provided to the national market is related by Capt. Joe Lore of Solomon's Island, along with an interview with his father, Capt. J. C. Lore Sr. from fifty years earlier.

Pepper Langley relished his days of establishing his own business after his high school commencement speaker told him he had a gold mine in his back yard.

The storytelling of Vi Englund is superb as she wrote vivid descriptions of going to sea. Get lost in the middle of roaring Atlantic storms in her ship's galley and appreciate the majesty of the sea.

Mark Robbins provides entertaining tales of sailing, and Cap'n Larry Jarboe cannot be beaten when it comes to knowing where the fish are hanging out and how to get them on your hook.

The Country Philosopher, Stephen Gore Uhler, got an elbow from another philosopher, Amos Arthur Holmes, but Steve wins overall for truthfulness, not a trait he learned from Jack Rue. Between Jack Rue and Fred McCoy, old tales are here for a new generation of tale-learners eager to find digital news of days of old. Some of the old gold mines of *The Solomon's Islander* and *The Chesapeake* have been reopened, and we found Tony Marconi and Lenny Rudow hiding back in the caverns, grinning and eager to share their news and views with the world.

The Bill Burton State Park at Cambridge, to the Cape Charles harbor shown on the cover, unite both shores of the Chesapeake to bring you, the reader, who may or may not dabble in U-Boat fantasies and time-warps, a complete view of the Tidewater region.

The Tidewater area contributed to the birth of Rock and Roll with the infamous home-grown talent of Link Wray, and Greg Laxton makes sure Link's place in history is secure.

No part of the Chesapeake lore could be complete without more Letters from Point Lookout Hotel, and while Alan Brylawski is now ninety-six, he refuses to join the Dead Poets Society. Alan tells you how to fix fried hard-crabs in great detail.

The Chesapeake region was important to the preparation for launching the successful offensives in both theatres of WWII, and John Peterson explains that effort.

Gail Whitney is a fervent chicken-necker, and she shares her best tips with all for a basket full of crabs.

Detailed follow-ups of the Pirate Poachers of the Bay are revealed by weak enforcement of Natural Resources laws. How these poachers get away with robbing the bounty of the Bay is disturbing and outrageous. Read what one prosecutor says should be done to get the outlaws behind jail bars and off of oyster bars in sanctuaries.

Thanks for joining us on the Chesapeake.

--- Ken Rossignol * Larry Jarboe

Additional books available in Kindle, paperback and Audible at Amazon and retailers worldwide

MURDER USA: True Crime, Real Killers

The Marsha & Danny Jones Thrillers

SIX KILLER THRILLER NOVELS - Marsha & Danny Jones Thriller
Series Books 1 – 6

Additional books by Ken Rossignol
Chesapeake 1850
Chesapeake 1880
Chesapeake 1910

Battle of Solomon's Island

Titanic Series
Titanic 1912
Titanic & Lusitania- Survivor Stories (with Bruce M. Caplan)
Titanic Poetry, Music & Stories

The Chesapeake Series
The Chesapeake: Tales & Scales (with Larry Jarboe)
The Chesapeake: Legends, Yarns & Barnacles (with Larry Jarboe)
The Chesapeake: Oyster Buyboats, Ships & Steamed Crabs
The Chesapeake: A Man Born To Hang Can Never Drown
The Chesapeake: Country Cornpone Cornucopia
The Chesapeake: Tidewater Sagas

Non-fiction
KLAN: Killing America
Panama 1914
The Story of The Rag
Leopold & Loeb Killed Bobby Franks (with Bruce M. Caplan)
Bank of Crooks & Criminals

CHESAPEAKE CRIME CONFIDENTIAL
Coke Air: Chesapeake Crime Confidential

PIRACY and PIRATES – Non-fiction
Pirate Trials: Dastardly Deeds & Last Words

Pirate Trials: Hung by the Neck Until Dead
Pirate Trials: Famous Murderous Pirate Book Series
Pirate Trials: The Three Pirates – Islet of the Virgin

Four Pirate Novels of Murder, Executions, Romance & Treasure - **Pirate Trials Series Books 1 – 4**

Fire Cruise
Cruising the Waterfront Restaurants of the Potomac

The Traveling Cheapskate series:
The Ninety-Nine Cent Tour of Bar Harbor Maine
Boating Chesapeake Bay

Chapter One

NAZI SCARE!

U-Boat Terrorizes
The Chesapeake Bay!
Krauts Sighted off Solomon's
Spies and Agents in Town!
Sub Fires on F-18!
The Solomon's Islander & The Chesapeake

(SPECIAL) SOLOMON'S ISLAND, MD. --- On a recent trip back from Tangier Island with a load of new crab traps for the coming season, Capt. Izzy Buckler reported being stopped in a sudden fog.

As the fog lifted, he found that his 38" bay built fishing boat was alongside a submarine. The men aboard the sub had machine guns aimed at him and his crew. They spoke exactly in a foreign language, which was recognized as German by Wally Hinckle, who is of German descent and could understand some of what the Germans were shouting.

It quickly became apparent to the men on the charter boat, Ellen A, that these people with the dangerous weapons trained on them were hostile and angry. Not knowing what the heck was going on, Solomon's men decided that the course of least assistance was their best hope of survival.

According to Captain Buckler, the Germans boarded their vessel, inspected it for arms, and brought forth five fishing knives, a signal flare gun, two .38 caliber pistols, and a double-barrel twelve-gauge shotgun.

Already knowing that they were in trouble as was, this was not the usual thing runs into on an average day. Izzy said that what really got them was when the German wanted to know what they had done with the depth charges.

Able to translate in a limited fashion, Wally told his fellow Marylanders that the German suspected them of being a small patrol boat and wanted to know why they did have any on their American Naval uniforms.

When Wally had told the Germans that they were not U.S. sailors, but only fishermen, the German Captain scoffed.

Just as the Germans were preparing to take their American prisoners aboard the U-Boat, as related by Captain Buckler, a U.S.

Navy F-18 screamed overhead, dipping low evidently to visually identify the vessel. As the plane swooped down, the German anti-aircraft gunner opened fire on the fleet's latest attack fighter. The fishermen reported that as the machine gun missed the plane, the jet circled around and was preparing to return fire, and suddenly, the submarine completely disappeared. "Where the Hell it went, we sure don't know! But away, it went!!" Exclaimed Capt. Buckler.

After the incident, Maryland Natural Resources Police patrol boats, hovercraft, and U. S. Navy search and rescue vessels from the Patuxent River Naval Air Station supplemented an extensive air search of the entire middle bay area for the U-Boat.

Photographs of the sub taken by the F-18 were rushed to the Pentagon by Helicopter for expert intelligence analysis. All comments from government agencies, including the Maryland State Police, Marine Police, NAS Pax River, and the sheriff's departments of St. Mary's and Calvert Counties, were evasive and non-committal. Privately sources from the government were mystified by the initial testimony of the fisherman from Solomon's and the U.S. Navy Pilot Lt. Cmdr. John Creighton, concerning the incident.

Finding the event impossible to deny, the authorities also have been reluctant to jump into the position of having t explain the mysterious appearance of a German U-Boat from World War II in the Chesapeake Bay.

Other reports of sightings are now starting to filter in from law enforcement agencies on the Eastern Shore of Maryland that had discounted earlier reports as the result of too much liquid refreshment by oystermen.

The only person willing to offer any type of opposition to the appearance of an apparent World War II-era submarine in the Chesapeake Bay 44 years after the war, has been Professor Donald P. Bucy of the Smithsonian Institution Center for Phenomena Study.

Dr. Bucy stated to *The Solomon's Islander*, "The current sun flares are causing extreme interference with radio signals. The breakdown of the ozone layer, and the high energy levels of the world during the war have been thought responsible for other unexplainable instances such as this".

The SICFPS has investigated has many such sightings since its information in 1979, but Dr. Bucy said, "Never before have we had such well-documented evidence such as the photos taken by the Navy pilot. We hope to see these pictures in a few hours at the Pentagon."

Solomons has had all available hotel rooms booked by the press, both national and international, and reporters and TV crews are hiring all available charter boats and are beginning their own searches.

It has been reported that one member of Capt. Buckler's crew, Sonny Bowen, picked up a German codebook that was dropped by the boarding officer from the marauding U-Boat. The CIA sent a helicopter down from Langley to retrieve the 44-year-old codebook. CIA spokesman Claude Fotheringham declined to comment on what the agency expected to learn from the codebook.

Most are not quite sure about what a "Time Warp" is, but they sure believe that the U-Boat was there in the bay. American patrolling of the Atlantic Coast and the Chesapeake during W.W. II was a major effort to prevent the landings of spies and agents on American soil during the war.

Already, some folks openly discussed the possibility of the German U-Boat having landed spies who are laboring under the impression that this 1944 and their own country is at war with America. Enemy agents with a mindset of wreaking havoc on our power system or other vital infrastructure in the America of 1989 could be a very real threat to our security. Officials are not commenting on this possibility, but there has been a noticeable step-up in police cruisers in all areas as well as undercover policemen in local restaurants and bars.

The March 5th incident has turned Solomon's upside down and may have changed our lives forever!

Chapter Two

The Blind Owl of Cypress Swamp

By John J. Peterson

Perched on its swing high in its cage, the unblinking eyes of the prison-stripped Barred Owl seem to focus on me and follow my movements with a fixed stare. I don't know that I anticipated anything unusual when, on the suggestion of Calvert County Staff Naturalist Andy Brown, I descended the hill behind the Cypress Swamp Visitors Center near Prince Frederick. After all, not being an Ornithologist (a student of birdlife), to me, an owl is an owl; they all sort of look alike, and they all make the same noise – hoot.

I wondered why this one bird would be captive while all others were free to fly at will.

Returning from the quarter-mile swamp tour, I questioned naturalist Brown on the purpose of the owl's isolation and noted its alertness in focusing on my every movement. It was only then that I learned that the owl was blind and that he was reacting to sound rather than sight.

It was the conservationist's concern for wildlife that the injured owl remained captive. "If we were to turn him loose," said Brown, "he wouldn't survive. Since the owl depends on other wild prey for survival, his eyesight is irreplaceable."

It seems that owls are as prone to be injured in automobile accidents as humans are. Staff Naturalist Mitzi Poole noted that the owl is more susceptible than other birds because of its restrictive vision.

"Owls are probably the most frequently automobile-injured bird and are often observed in an apparently dazed condition alongside the roadways," explained Poole. "Their eyes are locked into their sockets in a forward-facing configuration unlike any other bird, but they have considerable rotation capability in their necks. When they're in pursuit of prey, they can only see straight ahead. We feel it's this restricted vision that causes so many of them to be struck by cars. When crossing a road, they can only see directly in front of them and cannot see approaching headlights in time to react.

"…owls are as prone to be injured in accidents as humans are…"

The staff believed that the owl was about two years old due to not having yet acquired hunting skills.

His blindness was discovered after the local veterinarian had pinned a broken leg and wing and was preparing to release him. The awkwardness of the owl led the vet to examine the bird's eye, and it was discovered that the eyes had been irrevocably damaged. The owl was hopelessly blind. The vet called the Center and advised the staff that she was aware of a bird requiring care for its survival.

Division Chief Dwight Williams emphasizes that the Center does not perform the functions of a zoo. "We keep only animals which could not survive on their own, for example, the permanently disabled," he said. "Frankly, we have no justification for maintaining and feeding injured animals other than as educational tools."

"Most visitors assume that owls "hoot" as a means of communication, and they'll try to get the bird to hoot," said Poole. "Unfortunately, this is a misconception because the language of the species varies. Actually, our blind owl becomes frightened when viewers innocently attempt communication with him because he hears sounds he doesn't understand. Because the owl is easily frightened, visitors are encouraged to view him accompanied by a member of the staff."

A visit with the blind owl in the company of one of the center's naturalists is to take an introductory course in wildlife. The Barred Owl is a large gray-brown, puffy-headed woodland owl with big moist brown eyes with streaks resembling bars across the chest and extending lengthwise on the belly. It has white spots on its back. It also differs from most owls except the Barn Owl lacking the yellow color of the eyes. Roger Tory Peterson, in his *Field Guide to the Birds*, describes a dozen species and notes that number worldwide to be one-hundred and thirty-four.

A nocturnal animal, a bird of the night, our Barred Owl, if free, would probably not leave Cypress Swamp since his natural habitats are woodlands, wooded river bottoms, and wooded swamps. His keepers describe him as a "rooster" since he roosts and makes his home in a tree's cavity. His sound is "Hoohoo-hoohoo-hoohoow" with the "aw" characteristic at the end. He may actually sound like the barking of a dog.

"We're a little reluctant to give him a name," said Mitzi Poole," for several reasons, "the primary one being frankly, we don't really know what its gender is, or whether it's he or she. We keep saying "he" because I believe we're inclined towards using this vernacular.

"Besides," she continued, "we've already had one embarrassing experience. The cage our owl is in originally built for a disabled bird. It had been shot and had a bad wing. We named "him" Skipper because he never flew and would skip around his cage. We thought we had correctly identified Skipper as a member of the masculine gender until one day, "she" laid an egg. We realized we'd made a mistake. To be honest about it, I wish we could name it instead of alternating "he," "she, and 'it's."

Actually, the owl can fly and do so gracefully, according to Brown. The problem is that he doesn't know where he is going and is always bumping into things. Occasionally, Andy will take him to Point Lookout for a taste or freedom but keeps him on a leash to prevent his flying away. "Other than for his blindness, he's a very healthy bird," says Brown.

One doesn't have to be an Ornithologist or a dedicated bird watcher to appreciate the experience of a visit with The Blind Owl of Cypress Swamp. The owl of itself is but a single bird, but it serves as an introduction to the various species of owl life and a natural resource seemingly out of place on the Eastern Shore. It's an attraction for young and old.

Chapter Three

Catfish Tacos

By Christy Henderson
Buzz's Marina

I just ran across the recipe I used the other day while cleaning the kitchen and thought I'd pass it on. We cut the catfish into longer strips vs. the chunks we normally do because we were putting it into taco shells, but I liked it in strips better than chunks anyway, I think.

I rolled the fish in Essence (Emeril's Creole Seasoning) which was:

2 ½ tablespoons paprika

2 tablespoons salt

2 tablespoons garlic powder

1 tablespoon black pepper

1 tablespoon onion powder

1 tablespoon cayenne pepper

1 tablespoon dried leaf oregano

1 tablespoon dried thyme

Combine all ingredients thoroughly and store in an airtight jar or container

The fish was wet, so it stuck really well.

I put House Autry fish fry in a baggie and dropped the fish in and covered it with the House Autry and then deep-fried.

It was splendid! Now that said, for me, it was just on the border of what I could tolerate spicy-wise, and my daughter said the same thing. I had LIBERALLY coated the fish with the Essence. Next time I might not coat it quite as much with that.

I didn't tell Heather it was catfish until the next day because I wasn't sure if she liked catfish or not, and if she didn't, I was afraid she wouldn't try it. She was SHOCKED. She said when they were out to sea on the carrier, they were served catfish a couple times a week, and this tasted nothing like the catfish she knew from the Navy. She REALLY liked this a lot.

I think prepared this way it would make a great sandwich. Michael thought it was the best fish taco he ever had.

Chapter Four

Moose Pie

By E. V. Roderick

Moose make pies just like cows do. If you don't know what a cow pie is, there's little this write can do to adequately describe them. Just journey through a cattle pasture and check out the circular brown lumps, drying in the grass.

Moose leave similar droppings in the Bush and Bogs of the North Country.

Studs and I acquired ownership of some acreage in Central Maine, and the following summer, we went there to survey the premises. While walking through our woods, what did I discover but – Moose droppings. Since Studs was a bit off walking, and I was so excited that a moose actually lived on our property, I decided to get the pie up and save it. What a perfect give for my honey – then to dry it, shellac the remains, and make it into a pen and pencil set for his office. He'd be the only guy in the office with one.

I carefully scoped that rascal up, put in on a cookie sheet, wrapped it in plastic, and smuggled it home when we returned.

The following day, to dry out the pie, I put it in my kitchen oven, set at 200 degrees Fahrenheit and then went over to my neighbors to gossip and watch the soaps. It was well over two hours when I came back through the backdoor to discover the house full of sweet, nutty aroma. This was certainly not what I expected; a cow's pie wouldn't have been so gracious. Since it was close to that time, my darling, Studs gets home I put the hot pie down in our cool walk-out basement for safekeeping. Then I never thought about it again until there was a knock on my front door two months later.

At the steps was a man, with a stern face, dressed in a suit and raincoat. He whipped out a bi-fold with a gold badge on one side and an ID card on the other side, which read in big red letters FBI.

Special Agent Smith wanted to know all about the

property in Maine, how many acres, what crops were farmed there? When was the last time we were there? Did we bring anything back?

Well, to say the least, I was thrilled to have a Special Agent so interested in our property. Until he intimated that something had been eating or picking a marijuana patch up there. Holy Smokes'. Somebody had been growing the stuff up there on our property, and now the Government thought it was us.

I assured S. A. Smith we weren't dopers and never used the stuff. Eventually, the FBI left, but not before commenting that Interstate Transportation of Marijuana is a Federal offense. It meant jail for at least a million years. Then out the door, Smith went.

No sooner did I close the front door, than a sweet, nutty smell comes to my nose. Then I remembered the moose dropping – that damn moose had probably been eating the reefer. If so, then the pie is still full of it, no wonder the particular smell. Or maybe my conscious was playing tricks on me.

Then another knock at the front door, and who should it be, no other than Agent Smith, FBI.

I started shaking, and then the tears streamed down my cheeks. I only vaguely remember blubbering about never seeing my kids again and leading the FBI downstairs. I uncovered the moose pie and held it out to Agent Smith.

He just stared at me with cold steel eyes, and then his expression softened almost imperceptibly.

"Just a minute Ma'am. There's a lot of undigested vegetable matter here. We better send it to the lab."

Agent Smith then pulled out a Ziploc bag, and I placed the moose pie inside. All kinds of FBI and Evidence, in big red-lettered labels, papers were attached to the bag. Smith sealed it up with a drop of crazy glue on the Ziploc.

I was sure this was the part where I'd be frisked, handcuffed, and led away. But not so, the FBI man said he'd call in a few days. "Don't leave town."

Studs got home that evening and asked me what was wrong. I was too quiet, then realizing that wasn't normal, I'd prattle on about nothing.

Studs knew something was wrong, but I wasn't telling. This kept up for two days when the phone finally rang, and it was the FBI.

"Well, Ma'am, the agent drawled, "I have some good news and bad news."

"The good news is that it's not marijuana." Silence on the phone lines."

"Yes, yes, what's the bad news?" I yelled.

"Well, Ma'am, it's chewed up the paper from a magazine called *The CHESAPEAKE.*

The State of Maine wants to talk to you about feeding wild animals strange substances.

Chapter Five

Growing up in Solomon's

Skipjacks on the Chesapeake

By Pepper Langley

In the last seventy years of my life, I have watched one of the greatest workboats ever on the Bay come and go. When I was a small boy in Solomon's, I would see hundreds of the large noble Skipjacks sailing in and out of Solomon's as they worked out on the Bay dredging oysters off the flats of the Bay.

These boats were very strong boats, and although they were considered heavy boats, they were good sailing boats in light wind. The Skipjacks were first noticed working on the Bay in the early 1800s and in the year of 1880 there were 700 vessels employed in dredging and better than 3,000 crew members sailing on these boats.

The Chesapeake Bay Skipjacks come up from the boats called Bateaux, they were smaller boats from 20 feet to 40 feet long and well-planked from stem to stern on the bottom or what they called forward and aft plank. The Skipjacks were approximately 40 feet to 70 feet long and were planked from chime to keel on the bottom or what they called herringbone plank. These boats carried two sails, one the jib sail and one mainsail. These sails were enormous for the size of the boats, but these Skipjacks have a very wide beam, which helps a lot in a good breeze of wind. The beam of the Skipjack is nearly 1/3rd the length of the hull, and the mainsail boom is the length of the boat so you can understand the large sail carried on these boats.

In my younger days as a boy I was very amazed at the large fleet of boats that laid up in Solomon's when they were working off from the Patuxent River and after working hours on the bay all day, it was a sight to see these boats tied or anchored in Solomon's Harbor.

One of our greatest amusements, was to meet at the old Webster Store, in the evening when the captains and crews all gathered there and sat around the old coal store and told stories of the day and also of days gone by, and we all loved to hear them talks of adventures during their lives as watermen.

To me, it is so sad to see these boats pass on and may soon be gone forever.

When you see the days when there were hundreds of them – then the days there were dozens of them, and now it is less than a dozen Oystering on the Bay today.

In the winter of 1987, I was invited down on board a Skipjack by the Captain of the boat.

I was there just as they were cooking their dinner and as you know most of these boats had a good cook and I can tell you this was true that evening as they had baked chicken, baked potatoes, hot rolls, coffee for desert they had cake and peaches and I could understand how hungry they were after a hard day's work.

There were two boats tied up together at the Lore Oyster House, which is part of the Calvert Marine Museum.

I was welcomed aboard and invited to have dinner with them, but as it was, I had already had my dinner, and I thanked them for their hospitality.

I spent about two hours that evening with these watermen. The crew of both boats had dinner on one boat together, as I was talking to these gentlemen, I was told that both boats were owned by kin in the same family and before I left each captain told me how their fathers and grandfathers did the same thing as they were doing, but they thought it would be their last year oystering on the bay as there were not enough oysters to pay expenses in upkeep and wages.

After leaving the boats and bid them goodbye. I had a good idea of what was happening to the remaining few Skipjacks on the bay.

When I arrived home, I just sat down and thought of the good old days of the Chesapeake Bay Skipjacks and the hard crew of watermen that sailed them.

Last winter, there were none come in the harbor, and I feel now that their days have passed on forever.

Skipjack under sail. Library of Congress

Chapter Six

Trained to Assault The Beaches; But Where?

By John J. Peterson

Special Correspondent for **The Chesapeake**
This is another in the series on the role of Solomon's as an amphibious training base during World War II.

With the establishment of the U.S. Naval Amphibious Training Base at Solomon's, there still existed a lack of consensus among the allies as to where the initial landing on Fortress Europe would take place. Although the assault would eventually take place in North Africa, this lack of agreement had to have its effects on the conduct of training exercises, and it's worth taking a few pages to point out the difficulties facing those charged with preparing ship crews and troops to lead the way.

As was pointed out earlier the first challenge for American strategists was to plan for the enormous movement of masses of men and equipment over long distances for amphibious landings, a challenge, therefore, untried in size and scope. Another was the need to train the crews that would "man" the vessels. The construction of the amphibious base at Solomon's been the first large-scale response to this requirement and receive its formal designation in July 1942.

But even while the training was underway, there was a lack of agreement on where the initial landing would be made. We had pointed out in preceding articles that there were three plans for invading axis-held territories: "Operation Sledgehammer," "Operation Roundup," and "Operation Torch," initially designated "Operation Gymnast" by the British, and the focus of much dissension among American and British military and political strategists.

The Americans were under considerable pressure from the Soviets to open up a second front that would force the Germans to withdraw 40 divisions from the Russian front in 1942. However, the American plan, with which the British had reservations, called for a concentration and massive buildup of material and troops in the British Isles under the code name "Bolero" in preparation for a cross-Channel assault upon the European Continent early in the Spring of 1943 to be called "Operation Roundup." Under the American plan, there would also be a limited assault across the Channel in September of 1942 if considered necessary to relieve pressure on the Russians, designated "Sledgehammer."

The British continued to oppose Sledgehammer raising many questions. Did the Americans have a plan? (So far the British had not devised one they felt could be successful.) Where would they strike? Are there landing craft and shipping available? Who would be in command? What British troops would be required in support? And finally, could the allies remain idle in the Atlantic throughout the whole of 1942 if Sledgehammer was not feasible?

To the last question, the British revived their "Operation Gymnast," the invasion of North Africa as the more acceptable plan. There was a good reason for concern in North Africa. Field Marshal Rommel and his Africa Korps had launched an all-out attack against the British Eighth Army, forcing a withdrawal of the main British strength from Libya and across the Egyptian border leaving behind in the coastal town of Tobruk some 33,000 troops and enough supplies for three months.

Again, this raised the question as to the practicality of Sledgehammer, the assault on the European coast to relieve the Russians. Could not the same argument be made in favor of Sledgehammer, a reprieve for the hard-press British troops in North Africa? There were also political and psychological gains to be made in "Operation Gymnast": the early employment of American troops, a boost to American morale, needed battle experience for the Americans, and as an encouragement to the Russians that the allies intended to do everything possible to assist them. American professionals were still skeptical, emphasizing the difficulties of moving troops and supplying them from the sea, not to mention the question of the strategic value of North Africa to the allies. Was it worth the cost? The forced withdrawal of the British Eighth Army by the troops of the Desert Fox did little to add to the British Argument.

On Sunday, June 21, 1942, in the Oval Office of the White House, Prime Minister Churchill was handed a message shocking him and the American President with the news that Tobruk, with its 33,000 troops, had fallen. All the advances the British had made over the past two months were wiped out. Global implications were that another major battle could destroy the British forces in Egypt, opening the way to the enemy of the entire Middle East. In addition to such a loss, it would mean the giving to the enemy of the Valley of the Nile and the Suez. It would raise questions as to how Chiang Kai-shek could be sustained in China and how sufficient material aid could be gotten to Russia.

By July, the British Eighth Army had retreated all the way to El Alamein, forty miles west of Alexandria, where it was spread dangerously thin along a thirty-five-mile front, and there was the fear of a linkage of powerful German forces coming down from the Caucasus with those coming up from Egypt. On July 8, Washington informed the British that it had decided not to launch Sledgehammer, the limited operation to relieve the pressure on the Russians. This was good news for the British because it meant the freeing of millions of tons of shipping to support the Sledgehammer. However, American military strategists still had concern over the effect the North African campaign would have on the scheduled Operation Roundup, the full-scale assault on the continent of Europe.

To relieve some of the acrimony that had entered into the discussion of the pros and cons related to the two operations, "Sledgehammer" vs. "Gymnast", semantics were injected and the British-proposed Gymnast was re-designed "Operation Torch", and it was Operation Torch that would be accepted as the first major strike against the Axis powers.

On August 13, 1942, a formal detective was sent to Lt. Gen. Dwight D. Eisenhower, who had been sent to England to assume overall command to proceed with Operation Torch. This brought to a halt consideration of Sledgehammer, the diversionary attack on Europe. The invasion was made up of three separate forces: 35,000 Americans embarked from the United States for French Morocco; 39,000 more left England to take Oran in western Algeria, and a third force of 10,000 Americans and 23,000 British sailed from Britain to seize Algiers. All were transported and protected by the U.S. and Royal navies.

Later Eisenhower would write. "The venture was new – it was almost new in conception. Up to that moment, no government had ever attempted to carry out an overseas expedition involving a journey of thousands of miles from its bases and terminating in a major attack."

On June 12, 1942, the U.S. Navy assumed the obligation to train the crews required for the amphibious assault on Fortress Europe. In July, the first group of assault and trainees was billeted as a new amphibious base at Solomon's, which would become known as "The Cradle of Invasion."

On November 8, 1942, less than six months later, Solomon's-trained boat crews were among the series of convoys numbering more than eight hundred warships and transports assembling along the African coast between Morocco to the south and Algeria to the west, disembarking troops on the Atlantic and Mediterranean shores.

Operation Torch was underway.

Chapter Seven

A Reel Fine Time

By Cap'n Larry Jarboe

As astute readers of THE CHESAPEAKE TODAY know, I keep a 20-foot long Shamrock cuddy cabin boat down in the Florida Keys on a trailer to continue my fishing addiction year-round. I generally launch out of Garden Cove Marina in Key Largo using their hoist, which keeps the trailer dry. The wheel bearings and brakes are not nearly as likely to seize up since they've had no bath in saltwater.

2014 marked the thirtieth birthday of my boat, which was built in 1984. Since the carbureted 302 Ford Performer is the original power plant, Florida law permits me to apply for an antique registration that is only five bucks a year. Needless to say, my antique inboard Shamrock is now officially registered as an antique.

Mostly I fish antique reels with my old boat. I have a couple Penn Senator 6/0 trolling reels and a Penn Senator 6/0 modified with a 12-volt Electra-Mate conversion for deep dropping. Also, a few Gold Penn 7500 SS spinning reels stand by for schoolie dolphin. However, the Gold Penn spinners are a bit large for reef and Yellowtail Snapper fishing, so I broke down and decided to actually purchase a new reel rather than bid on and wait for delivery of another classic Penn reel through eBay. Unfortunately, the new Penns are built with Chinese bearings and components. Enough said.

While on the quest for the perfect reel through the halls of K-Mart and local tackle shops, I stopped dead in my tracks at a bulk purchase display of WaveSpin DH4000 reels at the Yellow Bait House. With the Florida tax, I walked away with one of those reels with the sawtooth design at the front of the spool for slightly more than forty bucks. This looked like a superb reef and Yellowtail Snapper reel if it will only hold up to saltwater usage.

Less than a month earlier, Catfish Bill Davis had out fished me big time on the Potomac River using this same reel. Now, I had my own to test.

Unfortunately, the blustery but warm weather only allowed me one trip out into what was even then very rough seas. After a trip to the edge of the Gulf Stream in a 5-6 foot close chop, I decided to fish the White Banks patch reef complex where the 3-4 foot seas were much more fishable in the 20-knot Northeast wind.

After catching and releasing a nice sized but out of season Red Grouper, I settled into filling the cooler with grunts, porgy, and yellowtail. The DH4000 reel worked smoothly, but I wondered how it would handle the salt spray that had saturated both the reel and my clothes.

Unfortunately, the gears in the reel stiffened up in just a day after brutal saltwater usage, whereas the old Penns continue to crank.

Capt. Justin Hopper of the Fantastic II, the top charter boat in Key Largo, spotted my saw tooth spool WaveSpin and asked me how I liked it. He had just picked up a few, especially for Yellowtail Snapper chumming. Great minds really do think alike.

I expressed my concerns about saltwater corrosion. His reply was to pack the reel with lube and keep it out of the spray. That's easily done on a 44' long custom charter boat. My Shamrock will soak you in a heartbeat.

So, I filled the DH4000 with WD-40 and ended up stripping out the lube hole screw as well as melting off the chrome paint on the heel of the reel. Needless to say, the WaveSpin reels are not ready for the big brutes in blue water. Still, the sawtooth spool design would actually work well on a reel with quality American stainless steel components.

Until someone comes up with that combo, I'll be searching eBay for the good old reel deals. Happy bidding!

Larry Jarboe - bass21292@yahoo.com

Catfish Bill Davis. Photo by Cap'n Larry Jarboe

Chapter Eight

I Bid You Farewell

The Country Philosopher - Stephen Gore Uhler

By Stephen Gore Uhler

I am old enough to fondly remember when my beloved Southern Maryland was renowned as being "The Land of Pleasant Living." Sorrowfully, it no longer exists and is only a cherished memory. It was destroyed by so-called "progress." In the name of "progress" our rural character has largely vanished; farmers and watermen made nearly extinct; the public schools reduced to academic mediocrity; the local economy foolishly addicted to a military base and government spending; our essential public services and facilities over-burdened by uncontrolled and irresponsible growth; and the cost of living, housing, and taxes made too damn high. What value is there to "progress" if it results in a lesser quality of life for people?

Life in St. Mary's County has steadily become more and more unpleasant, and it will only get worse. But, not for my family and me.

This is my last commentary column. My thanks to Ken Rossignol for giving me the opportunity to publicly state my opinions for the last 14 years.

My compliments to him for having the courage and tenacity, despite great difficulties and opposition, to provide the people of this county with a newspaper that is unafraid to report what people have a right to kno but would otherwise be denied them. Knowledge is power, and the powerful people who run this county for their own greedy purposes would prefer that you be ignorant.

I will not be here for next year's local elections. My opponents will surely rejoice at this news. It will be the first time since 1990 that my name will not appear on the ballot for a county commissioner election in St. Mary's County. My voice of opposition to politics-as-usual controlled by self-serving special interests will no longer be heard. My sincerest thanks to the many thousands of concerned citizens who voted for what I stood for. There were just not enough of you.

As for the many who seek elected offices, beware of those whose political and personal interests and ambitions are of greater importance to them than serving public interests. Wisely elect people who would be your public servants and reject those who are simply the surrogates of the local Good-old-boys, both Republicans and Democrats.

From 15 years of first-hand experience, I can attest to the fact that local political and public affairs are a culture of corruption. I have also learned that it is truly a curse to be public-spirited. But, I take solace in knowing that over time, my positions on public issues have been largely validated by the course of events. I can tell you all, "I told you so!" Now, you must live with the consequences.

St. Mary's County, which could have continued to be a special place to live, is well on its way to becoming just like Prince George's County, a hideous transformation that I most earnestly wanted to prevent.

Thankfully, I will not be here to see it. I offer these words as an epitaph in memory of what was once "The Land of Pleasant Living": "Sadly, no one reached out to save it while still there was time to do so."

As for me, it is a far, far better place to which I now go. I depart St. Mary's County and Maryland with no regrets. Actually, I feel sorry for the people of this county and state. By your idiotic willingness to complacently accept political and public corruption and injustice, you provide the means by which you suffer. As you watch St. Mary's County go to Hell, you have no one to blame but yourselves.

I BID YOU FAREWELL.

Chapter Nine

Letter From Point Lookout Hotel

By Alan Brylawski
Special Correspondent for The Chesapeake

Well – The old Hotel is gone! Torn down in what should have been the prime of its life. It was built in 1929, which should have been made it 60 years old, had it been allowed to stand. BUT, it had become old and decrepit – so it had to go. What scares me is, that's just how my wife described me the other day. I hope she wasn't too upset when I told her that I wasn't quite ready to go just yet. Thinking back on it, she did seem a might put out – think I better sleep with one eye open?

Speaking of being or feeling old – nothing, BUT NOTHING, will bring home the passing of years more than attending your High School graduating class's 50th REUNION!

It was quite an affair! Not only was it our 50th, but it was also FIRST!! Can you beat that? Not having seen hardly any of the kids you graduated with for fifty years and then getting together for a couple of nights of "whoop it up." Just like the old days, eh? Not quite!

The shindig was held at the Hyatt Regency in Bethesda, Maryland (not a plug – but it was rather nice). My wife and I stayed at the Hotel for the two nights despite the fact that Jean did not feel tiptop (perhaps the understatement of the year). Her operation, plus a stubborn headache (this time it wasn't me), made her just a touch grouchy in the beginning.

I think while we were checking in, her sense of humor broke through the clouds. There, walking in front of us, was an elderly man with a very pronounced limp.

I was shocked to hear my "baby face" remark," Oh look, I'll bet He is one of your old classmates – HE WALKS JUST LIKE YOU!

Before I could think of a withering retort, I sorrowfully heard the gentleman ask, "Where is the 50th reunion of Woodrow Wilson High School cocktail party?" Right then and there, I had an inkling that I probably wouldn't recognize and or remember a single solitary soul. I think I mumbled something about going to bed. My "better half" would have none of that (her grin was ever so slightly devilish). "You know how I am about names!!" She nodded and grinned some more. I will never take her out of a sickbed again.

Just before entering the room where the first night's festivities were being held, we were both given LARGE name tags. Mine had a picture of a black-haired dark-complected, rather handsome boy on it. I started to say that I had the wrong label when it dawned on me that had been me Lo so many years ago. Gad, the picture was from our yearbook! It even had the dumb stuff printed under the picture. I was NEVER called "SHORTY"! "Devilish" or "Man-about-town" maybe, but NEVER Shorty"!!

I was never called Shorty ...

As I entered the room, I knew why we had "oversized" tags on. The first person I encountered quickly put on his glasses as I approached, bent his head to peer intently at my tag - almost hitting my chin with the top of his head while he mumbled: "Alan – so good to see you"!

After that, I took pity on people. If they looked at me with that "should I know you look," I stuck out my hand and announced in a firm voice, "I used to be Alan Brylawski." Wish the hell they had done the same for me – it was hard getting close enough to those SMALL name tags to see who I was talking too.

Good Lord! That old woman I was just talking to was one of the old girlfriends! What has happened to all these people? My wife reminded me later that I didn't endear myself to some of my classmates when I complained rather loudly upon entering the room, "Why are all these OLD people here?"

AND THEN – in came three guys I could hate for the rest of my life – in fact, I fully intend to! Their names won't mean anything to you, but I shall name them out of pure arrogance.

First, there was "Jimmy Schwab" – the ONLY thing that changed about him was his hair was now snow white! He still stood tall, erect, and handsome. He didn't need a name tag! Everybody knew who he was the instant he came into the room! Then there was "Stanley Elman," his forehead was a scouch higher than fifty years, but that was it!! Not a line on his face. The worst of all was "David Wise" – NOTHING HAD CHANGED! Shades of Dorian Gray!

I wonder if he has HIS picture in the attic? Not only did he look like he just stepped out of our yearbook, BUT he ACTED like it! I had trouble doing a waltz, and there he was "jitterbugging."

Without question, you can understand that HE is the easiest to hate – right?

All in all, everybody who attended had a good time. It was great fun trying to see how many you could really remember. I was amazed and rather pleased at my ability. As I remember it, I only insulted a few by telling them I didn't have the foggiest notion which they were (even after they told me!) My wife said that I behaved myself not as good as she wished but better than she hoped. I guess that was a compliment?

If we have another reunion, I told them I thought we shouldn't wait another fifty years – When I asked, "What the hell is so funny about that?" my wife kicked me in the shins. I don't think I will take her to the next one.

May all your reunions be happy ones.

Till next time.

Chapter Ten

LINK WRAY AND THE RAY MEN

- Rock and Roll Pioneers –

By Greg Laxton
The Chesapeake

Although he received the lion's share of the accolades, guitar legend Link Wray was actually powered by three cogs in one machine. Brothers Vernon and Doug Wray were instrumental (pun intended) in helping to make Link Wray what he became – the founding father of rock and roll guitar.

Garage, punk rock, grunge, heavy metal, rock guitar, in general, ...they can all trace their roots to Link Wray.

The Wray Brothers came from humble beginnings in Dunn, North Carolina. Sons of half-Shawnee street preachers, the brothers, had a hard life. The first decade of their life was spent in poverty. Link put it best when he said, "Elvis came from welfare, I came from below welfare."

Vernon Aubrey Wray was born on on January 7, 1924. Fred Lincoln "Link" Wray came along May 2, 1929. Rounding out the trio was brother Douglas Leon, born Independence Day, 1933.

The family lived near the local fairgrounds in Dunn. When Link was 8, he scrounged up brother Vernon's guitar and was sitting on the family porch, trying to hammer out a few rudimentary chords. A traveling African American carny worker who went by the name of "Hambone" happened by and taught Link the sound of the blues. When Hambone began to play some bottleneck slide guitar, Link knew then what he wanted to do.

In 1942, the family headed north to the shipyards of Portsmouth Virginia, where Link's daddy had found work. The beginnings of the Wray Men came to be when the brothers formed a band and played Western Swing – or as Link put it, "rock and roll before it was rock and roll." In the Navy town of Portsmouth, there seemed to be a bar or club on every corner, providing plenty of opportunities for work.

The band consisted of brothers Vernon on vocals and rhythm guitar, Link on lead guitar, Doug pounding the skins, and "cousin" Brantley "Shorty" Horton playing doghouse bass. For a short time, Dixie Neal played pedal steel. Dixie's brother was Jack Neal of Gene Vincent's Blue Caps.

Band names changed according to the venues they played... Lucky Wray and the Palomino Ranch Gang... Lucky Wray and the Lazy Pine Wranglers and a couple more. ("Lucky" was Vernon, who had picked up his moniker from his success at the local card tables).

Always the entrepreneur, Vernon held the first taxi license in Portsmouth. Vernon and Link drove a cab during the day – nights were spent honing their craft.

In 1953, the brothers were invited to play as part of a tribute show in Montgomery, Alabama. It was there they saw Curtis Gordon perform, and the girls going wild. Curtis wasn't playing country, he wasn't playing the blues...Link and Vernon concluded, "there's something happening here." The boys arrived home and continued to experiment, recording some new sounds.

The band, minus Dixie, headed to Washington DC in 1955. During that time, the DC area was a hotbed of country music. They shared the stage with the likes of Roy Clark, the Jaguars (featuring a young rocker named Charlie Daniels), Marvin Rainwater, Patsy Cline, and many more all throughout Washington DC and Southern Maryland.

1956 saw the first rumblings of the brothers on wax, with rockabilly and country sides from Lucky on Starday Records, and Link's first vinyl etchings on Kay, a record company run by Ben Adelman who was the owner of Empire Studios in Washington. Link's first record was a split EP featuring two early rockabilly recordings by Link – "Johnny Bom Bonny" and "I Sez Baby." These records were released when the band was in DC, but the recordings came from those home recording sessions in Portsmouth in 1953!

The band's career was interrupted when Link and Doug came down with tuberculosis and were placed in a TB hospital in Maryland. Link had picked up the disease during his stint in the Army during the Korean War. He passed it along to Doug.

With Link and Doug in the hospital with TB, Vernon struck out as a teen idol, landing a recording contract with Cameo Records. He was renamed Ray Vernon by the powers-that-be and molded as a pop singer in the Pat Boone / Perry Como vein. From here on, family and friends refer to Vernon as "Ray."

Doug would fully recover from his bout with TB. Link's condition was far more serious. His odds were not good. Link recalls, "I was coughing up blood in the death house. They were waiting for me to die". When doctors concluded the only way to save his life was surgery, the family rallied, and everyone prayed. Link pulled through, but his bout with TB cost him a lung. The docs told him to stick to playing guitar and forget about singing. Link told 'em, "it will take a higher power than you to tell me that."

Link was able to get a medical pass from the hospital to play guitar on brother Vernon's Cameo sessions. This resulted in Vernon's hit "Evil Angel" and "Remember You're Mine" (alternately released with the flip side "I'll Take Tomorrow Today" in 1957). Pat Boone took "Remember You're Mine" to greater success a short time later.

Link worked tirelessly to build up his health and singing voice while also refocusing on his guitar work. Link's experimental guitar sound became the anchor of the band, now rechristened "Link Wray and the Ray Men." Matched with Doug's heavy drumming and Vernon's production work, the brothers found that "something new" they first recalled back at that Hank Sr. tribute concert.

Like many bands in DC, Link, and the Ray Men were taken under the wing of Milt Grant. Milt was the host of "The Milt Grant Show," a record hop broadcast daily after school on WTTG-TV in Washington. The Ray Men were regulars, later becoming the house band and performing countless times on the show. Vernon hosted when Milt was out of town, and later had "The Ray Vernon Show," weeknights at 7:30.

Link struck gold - a gold record - with the instrumental "Rumble." The legend of "Rumble" is a curious one. Link himself has told varied stories of how "Rumble" came about. The most popular may be the story of Link and the Ray Men backing up The Diamonds at a Milt Grant Record Hop. According to Link, Milt asked the band to play the Diamonds hit "The Stroll." Link told Grant, "I don't know, no stroll." Brother Doug started hammering a stroll beat, and Link has said it was then that his "Jesus God" zapped "Rumble" into his head. On impulse, Vernon mic'd the amps. The kids went wild, and they played the song four times that night.

As legendary as that story is, historical records reveal the record hop was held on July 12, 1957. No mention of The Diamonds appearance can be found in any available advertisements for the Record Hop that night. Perhaps a bit more accurate is the story Link told to a UK magazine in 1978 –

"I was doing all these record hops for the kids with my brother doing most of the singing. One night in Fredericksburg, Virginia, a few of the kids got together and decided to do a little fighting. I started playing these notes as sort of a joke, but the kids came up to me afterward and said, 'Hey I like that sound, play it again.'"

"So I started playing and developing it until it sounded pretty good. The kids started asking for it because they liked it, so I went into the studio and recorded it. "

"Actually my brother was recording for Cameo Records at the time so at the end of one of his sessions I just went in and recorded two songs, "The Rumble" and a flip side "The Swag" – it cost 57 dollars."

This timeline would mean that "Rumble" was recorded at the end of Vernon's Cameo session for the rockabilly rave-up "I'm Countin' On You" and the flip "Terry (You're Askin' Too Much).

The working title of the tune was "Oddball." The fellas were always experimenting - pencil holes were punched in the tweeters of Link's amp, in an effort to duplicate that "dirty sound" they got on stage with the mic'd amplifiers that night in Fredericksburg. This historical session marked the first recording of intentional distortion in rock and roll. He didn't know it then, but with "Rumble," Link Wray invented the "power chord" - the key element popular in many styles of rock and roll.

Grant shopped the demo recording to Archie Bleyer of Cadence Records. He hated it, but his teenage daughter loved it. The song was renamed "Rumble," as Archie's daughter said it reminded her of West Side Story.

Rumble – an instrumental - was banned in Boston and New York for being "too suggestive" and for fear that it would incite teenage gangs to fight. Dick Clark wouldn't mention the title of the song when the band played it on American Bandstand. (You can't get much more "rock and roll" than that!)

Fearful that Link and the Ray Men would corrupt the morals of American youth, Archie Bleyer was done with them after "Rumble." They moved on to a major label deal with Epic Records resulting in the now-classic "Link Wray and the Wraymen" LP. Vernon continued to work with the Ray Men, but having opened a recording studio a few years earlier, he moved "behind the scenes" as the band's manager and producer of their recordings.

The band had a chart hit with "Rawhide," but Link tired of Epic's efforts to clean him up and put him in a Duane Eddy mold. Link said at one point Mitch Miller put him in front of a 40 piece orchestra – it took him half an hour to find his guitar. So the Ray Men walked away.

The brothers then formed one of the first "do it yourself" record labels – Rumble Records – in 1961. Vernon moved his recording studio from Washington DC down to his spread off Livingston Road in Accokeek, Maryland, in December 1962. The first stop was in the basement of Vernon's home.

Some of the Ray Men's most prolific work happened in the mid-1960s at Vernon's home in Southern Prince Georges County, Md. At the end of each night's gig in and around Washington, the band regrouped in Accokeek and recorded until daybreak.

All of Link's classic songs were recorded there. While the band was on the road, Vernon was fast becoming the "Sam Phillips of DC," as too many musicians to count spent time with the tape running in Accokeek.

Too busy (and too loud!) for his wife Evelyn, Vernon moved the studio across the street in a building that housed Wray's Market (always the entrepreneur...). Finally and most famously, the studio ended up in an outbuilding on the property and was christened "Wray's Shack 3 Tracks".

From the mid-1960s to 1970, Link Wray was a regular at many clubs, firehouses, high schools, and other functions in and around St. Mary's, Charles, and Calvert Counties. In one such interview, Link has mentioned the "Two Thieves Club, down by the water." (If anyone remembers this place, please get in touch!)

In 1970, the brothers were "rediscovered," and each signed to a 3 record deal with Polydor. For reasons yet to be determined, the only contract honored was Link's, resulting in his "back to the roots" critically acclaimed LP, "Link Wray." This record, like everything else, was a family affair with Doug playing drums as well as some acoustic guitar. Vernon handled the recording, backup vocals, and some rhythm guitar work.

"The Shack" was a busy place. The last recordings in Accokeek saw major label interest - Mordecai Jones and Link's solo debut on Polydor Records, as well as the UK issued "Beans and Fatback," studio outtakes of the "Link Wray" LP.

In 1972, Link and Vernon headed west to Tucson to "mellow out" and become one with the earth. Brother Doug stayed behind and continued cutting chops at his successful barbershop in Waldorf, Maryland, while still playing gigs at local clubs. He passed away in 1984.

Realizing what a special place "The Shack" was, Vernon had chopped off the back wall and took it with him to Arizona as a talisman of sorts. He used the wall to reconstruct The Shack and then continued his production work with Tucson musicians. He also wrote jingles for local businesses and released his final two recordings – "Superstar at My House" and "Wasted." Now incredibly rare, these recordings command top dollar among collectors. Vernon also pursued an acting career, landing parts in "Alice Doesn't Live Here Anymore" and four episodes of "Gunsmoke." He passed away in 1979.

After completing his contract with Polydor, Link hooked up with another DC musician, rockabilly singer Robert Gordon in 1977. This resulted in two major label LPs, "Robert Gordon with Link Wray" and "Fresh Fish Special," as well as world tours. Photographers missed one of the best moments in rock and roll history when both Bob Dylan and punk rocker Sid Vicious met Link backstage at a UK gig to pay homage.

In 1979, Link struck out on his own and never looked back. Shortly after that, Link moved to Denmark. He returned to the states for a tour in 1985. Link eventually relocated permanently to Denmark, where he continued to record and sporadically tour overseas. He would not come back to the States for a dozen years.

Throughout the '90s, Link Wray found new fans with his music being featured in such big-budget movies as Desperado, Independence Day, Pulp Fiction, 12 Monkeys, This Boy's Life, and others.

1997 saw Link return to American soil with the release of a new studio LP, a club tour and a return to national TV, with an appearance on "Late Night with Conan O'Brien" almost 40 years after playing "Rumble" on "American Bandstand."

The beginning of the 21st Century saw the release of "Barbed Wire," Link's last LP - and one of the most interesting of his career. It featured "Link unplugged" – several cuts of just Link's vocals and an acoustic guitar – half a century after the TB doctor told him he'd never sing again.

Link continued to return to the States every year or so for the remainder of his life, playing his "wild rock and roll." He toured until the end, playing 40 dates in the states in 2005. He passed away at 76 in November of that year.

———————

Though the main players in this story have passed, interest in Link Wray and the Ray Men is stronger than ever.

Link has been recognized as one of the "100 Greatest Guitarists" by Rolling Stone magazine. Guitar Player magazine cited "Rumble" as one of the Top 50 "guitar sounds" of all time.

Link and the Ray Men have been inducted into the following Halls of Fame – the Washington Area Music Association, Southern Legends, and the Native American Music Hall of Fame. There is a petition drive underway to get Link inducted into the Rock and Roll Hall of Fame.

In 2009, Link and the Ray Men's "Rumble" was added to the National Recording Registry by the National Recording Preservation Board, housed in the Library of Congress.

In 2010, brother Link was a featured artist in "Up Where We Belong" - an exhibit housed in the Smithsonian Institution's Museum of the Native American Indian in Washington, DC. This exhibit featured an ultra-rare video featuring a performance of the original Ray Men - Link, Doug, Shorty, and Vernon - that has not been seen since it was first broadcast over half a century ago on American Bandstand. This exhibit is currently on display in New York.

2011 brought the re-release of Vernon's final work, "Wasted." As with the original issue, it's limited to 1000 vinyl LPs.

Link and the Ray Men have influenced the likes of Bob Dylan, Neil Young, Pete Townshend, and thousands of guitarists the world over. Neil Young has said if he could travel back in time to see one band, it would be Link Wray and the Ray Men.

More recently, a highlight of the award-winning documentary

"It Might Get Loud" features Jimmy Page, citing Link as an influence as he spins a 45 of "Rumble" and turns back into a 16-year-old kid playing air guitar in his music room.

What does the future hold for Link Wray and the Ray Men? A documentary is currently in production, and a movie is rumored to happen. Long lost recordings have been unearthed and may be released in the not too distant future. Link Wray and the Ray Men just keep rumblin' on!

LINK LINKS:l

For more on Link Wray – www.LinkWray.com For more on Vernon Wray – www.VernonWray.com Sign the petition! www.InductLinkWray.com

LUCKY & LINK WRAY   Personal Manager   1129 Vermont Ave N.W.
                              Ben Adelman   Washington, D.C.

Chapter Eleven

A Solomon's Boy in a New Venture

By Pepper Langley

When I graduated from Solomon's High School, the first thing I thought of was getting a good job, but jobs were hard to find at that time. I had been warned by my doctor after having rheumatic fever at the age of seventeen that I would always have to do very light work for the rest of my life.

After thinking this over, I knew I had always liked artwork, and has I had been in sign painting since I was sixteen, I thought that would be the best field to go into. I had a small shop at my home place that I could work in, so I thought I would just as well get in the sign business, which I did.

After I got started and the local business found out that I was doing it, I soon began to get all the business that I could handle. Not only signs, but all boats had to be painted, and the numbers put on the bow every spring. I soon had so much work I could hardly handle all of it without working up into the night.

During the daylight hours, when the boatyards would haul the boats out, they would call me to come to letter the boats while they were on the railway. That made it easier for me, although I lettered as many in the water as on the railway. It seemed as though more sign painting and boat lettering I did, the faster I could do it. So, you see if a person in this business does not get fast, he cannot make a good day's work.

When I started out lettering boats, I was charging only $2.50 per boat – that was for six 3" letters on both sides of the boat, but I could paint a set in 10 minutes and walk away. So, if I painted 5 sets of letters a day, I was making $12.50 a day. I was doing pretty good at painting and making signs in my shop because at that time, most men with families were living off the water or in the shipyards.

Along with my own business, I got a job at the M. M. Davis Shipyard on Solomon's Island, and they were paying me twenty-eight cents per hour when I first went there. I thought for a while, I would have to pay them to let me work there, but I could make it up when I came home in the evening. I did want to learn a shipbuilders trade, which I did spend the first sixteen years of my life working in shipyards along with my sign work. It worked out alright as long as I could work eight hours in the shipyard and at least four hours in my own shop when I got home. Some of the places of business I painted for in Solomon's were the Standard Oil Co., Calvert Ice Co.; Webster Store; Evans Pier; Rekord Hotel; Bowen's Inn; Solomon's Yacht Club; Leon Langley Fishing Fleet; Woodburn's Seafood Co.; J. C. Lore Seafood and all the trucks used in the oyster business. I painted many other vehicles at that time and did work for many other marinas in later years. During WWII, the U. S. Coast Guard forced every boat owner to change the size of the letters on the bow of their motorboats to 24-inch letters – that was no harder to paint on, but it took longer!

It happened so quick and at short notice that I could not take care of all the large letters. Many boat owners painted their own letters on the boats.

I will never forget there was a barber in Solomon's who thought he could paint his own letters on the bow of his boat. He leaned over the bow and painted his numbers upside down. Guess what, he was never required to change them, but it was a good laugh. Many boats I lettered had names like "Thomas's Mink,"; "Katie Did,"; "My Love,"; and many more that had a lot of thought in them.

In the shipyard, I lettered the Manitou that later was President Kennedy's yacht, also the White Cloud, a large racer – the Ko-Asa, Lord Jim, Blue Moon, Cheerio I and Cheerio II, and Cheerio Three. I also lettered General Patton's yacht, the "WHENANDIF." This is just a few, but I could list so many more. I have thought over the years of many boats and thought how many there were, most were done in 23 K Gold Leaf. Now, since I retired, my son Jimmy took over my sign work, and what time he is not working at his full-time job at the Calvert Marine Museum, he is lettering and Gold Leafing many more boats than I did because there are ten times more boats in Solomon's now than when I was lettering.

At the commencement exercises, when I graduated from high school, the guest speaker was Theodore McKeldin, who, in later years, was Mayor of Baltimore and the Governor of Maryland.

I will never forget his words he said in his speech he made that night, and I will quote: "Never go out in the world searching for a gold mine when you may have one at your back door."

I have never seen a day that I could not make a good living in my shop, not far from my back door.

The Manitou was lettered by Pepper Langley when it was built at Davis Shipyards on Solomon's Island, Md. The yacht was donated to the Coast Guard and used by JFK. Photo JFK Library.

Chapter Twelve

Under the Blarney Stone

By John R. O'Meara

Fifty years ago, as I approached my twelfth birthday, my father drove me from our summer home at Breezy Point Beach to a farmhouse overlooking Chesapeake Beach and the Bay. He disclosed to me the location of a time capsule buried in the year 1890 by his grandfather. He instructed me to return to this spot in the year 1990 and excavate the capsule. He also entrusted me with the location of the map that would guide our descendants to this family treasure in the even event we did not survive the date.

The old house was deserted when I went to unearth the capsule in early January 1990. The map indicated I would find it beneath the back porch and under a good-sized piece of limestone with the date 1446 carved on it. I wish I had taken something more substantial than my old bricklayer's trowel to dig with because what I found buried there under the stone was a fair-sized lead-lined box that contained quite a few historical items, including a jar that somehow seemed to be hermetically sealed.

I later learned that the jar contained a stack of letters written by my great-grandfather, John O'Meara. The first letter I read, to my great surprise, was addressed to me. The letter revealed that my great-grandfather had instructed his son, John Dominic O'Meara, to bury this box in Calvert County, Maryland. Further that he was to instruct his not yet born son (to be named Raymond Michael O'Meara) to name his first-born son John Raymond O'Meara and that his great-grandson was to open the box in 1990.

This letter also informed me that the limestone bearing the 1446 date was indeed a piece of the original Blarney Stone from the Blarney Castle in County Cork, Ireland. Now Irishmen almost always tell the truth, so I will have to accept this as Gospel.

Great-granddad revealed in this first letter that the "potato famine" of the late 1840s in Ireland had eventually forced him to come to America to start a new life. After years of oppression by the English, he sought the capital city of this nation that had won its independence from the British.

The "Free State" of Maryland is where he finally determined he wanted to re-establish his family name, which dated to the early

Kings of Ireland. In particular, Calvert County, with its magnificent river and bay along with rolling hills, reminded him of home.

He advised me to go easy with the native population in Calvert County because they're decidedly English roots did not welcome Irish invaders from the areas that had broken off from Calvert to establish their own Counties.

His son, John Dominic O'Meara, was already acquiring land in the northern part of Calvert County, Md., and would use the wealth he acquired from his soft drink and beer bottling business in north-east Washington, D.C. to begin the development of Chesapeake Beach. Note: John Dominic would later own and operate the Chesapeake Beach and Amusement Park which was lost as a family possession by his death and the absconding of his lawyer in 1911.)

To digress from the contents of the letters for a while, I need to tell a little more recent history. My father, Raymond Michael O'Meara, known to his friends as "Mike," was orphaned in 1911 and placed in an orphanage in Washington, D. C. He was driven by a passion for continuing the family name in Calvert County. In spite of losing his laundry business during the Depression and raising four children, he finally acquired a home in Breezy Point Beach in the early 1940s.

Our family spent the summers and weekends at Breezy Point beginning in the 1930s by renting from Sam Peach and then at our parent's house until their deaths in 1956 and 1957. My sister, Jeanne Billhimer, continued to live at the house in Breezy until she married and moved to Chesapeake Beach.

Dad always urged me to establish roots in the County, and I purchased property in the Chesapeake Ranch Club in 1960 and built my home on Mill Creek in 1976.

I guess the whole point of this article is that not much has changed in the past one hundred years. Counting my oldest son, Tom, who lives in Lusby and his son, Patrick, six generations of O'Meara men have lived in Calvert County, and we are still considered "new people." We came here as everyone else, by water. So the only people who are real natives are the Indians we displaced. And those Indians were probably Irish descendants because you know how they acted when you gave them whiskey.

We "new people" now constitute a majority in Calvert County, and I am sure that we do not want to change any of the good things we found when we moved here. We only want to work, play, and worship with the same rights of ownership as others.

There are a few more stories in those letters under our piece of the rock, and given the opportunity, I may be able to let you sort out the "Blarney" from the truth and fiction.

Till then, I leave you with the Irish Blessing – "May the road rise to meet you, may the wind always be at your back. May the sun shine warm upon your face, the rains fall soft upon your fields, and until we meet again, may God hold you in the palm of his hand."

An outing from Walter Reed to Chesapeake Beach, Md.

Chapter Thirteen

The Duke of Solomon's

By Mark Robbins

The first time I ever heard of Solomon's Island, I was in the Solomon Islands in the Pacific, talking to a tall (about 6'5") slender (160 lbs.) young naval officer whose real name was Marmaduke but was call The Duke.

He said he was from somewhere around Solomon's Island and thought it was just about the prettiest place he ever saw. In The Duke's view, Solomon's Island was a whole lot better than the Solomon Islands. This was during the Korean War, and both of us were in Solomon's on leave from our ships. He left the day I arrived. We talked for less than an hour. He was as impressive as few men are; he projected maturity and integrity as well as a personal warmth that was far beyond his years. I wouldn't see him before he made history in Virginia and became a legend in his own time.

Months later, in Dam Neck, Virginia, the Duke reported for duty to the Fighter Air Defense Training Command, where I was assigned as a gunnery instructor. Duke was there to learn how to use and then instruct how to use the Navy's then-new radar-controlled 5 inch 70 anti-aircraft gun.

We bunked together while he was at FADTC. That's how I got to know him so well. That's why it was easy for me to understand (well almost) what he did later. The others, the ones that lost that $1,000 bet, did not understand, but I can guaran-dam-tee you that they will never forget The Duke and what he did that day. I think The Duke made them grow up some and see how a man is supposed to act.

Maybe the other instructors assigned to the base were jealous envious of The Duke. Maybe he made them feel uneasy because he always knew what he was doing. He always did his work efficiently, silently. He was polite but did not feel the need to socialize. He did his work, he went home and read or wrote letters.

Often we talked together about what his plans were after the war. He had several ideas on what kind of career he wanted, but the one thing that was always firm in his planning is that he would return to Southern Maryland, to Solomon's Island. It was really easy to respect a man who was so doggone sure of what he wanted to do. I was sort of envious because my own post-war plans were up in the air.

I think maybe the others, well most of them, did not cotton to The Duke because of his manner. He was aloof, but in a friendly way, I thought. He went to church every morning, and he read the Bible every night before he went to bed. He was great friends with the priest, where he went to Mass. They played cribbage together one night every week. One week they played at the church and the next they played at the Base.

In almost no time at all, The Duke had caught the Captain's eye. He was given the most important assignments, and it was to the Duke that the Captain turned when there was an emergency. Whatever their reasons, the other gunnery instructors, the other four besides myself, did not like The Duke. I think they suspected he was superior, smarter than they and did his job better, and on top of all that, he was in with the Captain, and they were out. They didn't know it then, but they were heading for a fall, a big fall in public – the kind of fall they would never, ever forget.

It all started one day when The Duke alluded as to how he used to shoot skeet with a .22 rifle and not the usual 12 gauge shotgun. Now that is some kind of shooting. There probably isn't one gunman in a million that could hit even one of those clay pigeons with a .22 rifle, let alone the two out of three that The Duke said he could. When he said that, the other instructors saw a chance to brand him a liar in public, and naturally, those four jealous joes could not resist the temptations. So they challenged him to a public skeet shoot to give him the opportunity to demonstrate his rare ability with a .22 rifle.

I just knew The Duke was on to them right from the start. In fact, I think maybe he planned the whole thing just to get money for his church.

Whatever he had in mind, I don't know for sure, but when these four cunning nerds made their challenge, The Duke accepted without hesitating long enough to bat an eye.

He wouldn't even consider it unless the bet was at least $100. Well naturally, the four fatuous fellows thought it would be the easiest $100 they had had ever made. They thought it was money in their pockets. They were even talking to everybody about how they were going to give a big beer bust with The Duke's money and not invite him to it. That's the kind of men they were – small and really mean. Even to this day, I get sort of sick when I think about them. On the other hand, I feel awfully proud, and I get all warm inside when I think of what The Duke did to them that day.

The big and unforgettable event took place on a Saturday morning. The four men, (I'm ashamed to say it, but they were all officers) had invited about two dozen friends to watch The Duke's public humiliation, his public branding as a braggart and a liar. On the other hand, The Duke had invited only two people – me and his friend the priest.

In the beginning, the Duke had said he would cover all the bets.

He didn't know the flakey four would try to persuade all their friends to bet against him. When he saw what they were doing, he said he wouldn't do it; that he would not take money from innocent people with whom had no quarrel. He the four flat out that that they could bet all they wanted and he would cover all their bets, but nobody else. And then repeated that he would not shoot a shot unless the bet were at least $100. These four men were so sure they were going to win, they got up $500 between them. Now mind you, $500 was a lot of money back then. The equivalent today would be in the thousands.

Just before this historic skeet shoot got started, The Duke did something that was really mean, but ever so glorious. He said he would hit more clay pigeons with his .22 than the best of them could hit with a shotgun. He put the screws to them when he also said that if he did not do better than his opponent with the shotgun, that he would give them double the amount of the bet ($1,000) provided they would they would give him double the amount of the bet if he did shoot better than his opponent.

So the bet came down to a shooting match between a shotgun and a .22 rifle. Each man would shoot at 26 clay pigeons, launched two at a time.

In the case of a tie, there would be another round of 26 clay pigeons.

It's all history now, and I am sure it will live forever in the folklore of the region, but I've just got to tell it like it was. The guy with the shotgun hit 25 of the clay pigeons.

Those four men just knew they were going to get $1,000 from The Duke. I just couldn't see how anybody could do better with a .22. I was watching their faces when The Duke began to shoot.

You wouldn't believe how their expressions began to change along about the 16th straight consecutive clay pigeon that The Duke had it. By the time he had hit 20 in a row, their eyes had grown wider and were filled with a kind of dark, gathering foreboding. They began to realize they might lose. When the last two clay pigeons were launched, the crowd of 30 to 40 people was as quiet as they would have been in church during service. The Duke did it with style. He hit both those last two saucers. He had waited a long time before he hit the 26th and winning clay pigeon. He waited until it was just a foot or two off the ground, then he popped it.

The crowd remained silent as the fulsome four paid The Duke $1,000 in cash. It was the saddest looking crowd I ever did see. They had come to see a public humiliation, and they had gotten their faces rubbed in the dirt. The Duke said nothing as he took the money. He just looked at them like they were a bunch of loathsome pack rats.

What The Duke did next was really the coup de grace. He turned to the priest, and right in front of that long-faced crowd, he said he wanted to donate the money, the whole $1,000 to the church. I just don't think there is a word, at least I can't think of it that would describe the expressions on those men's faces. That's how come I know that those four jerks will remember The Duke forever, even long after the pain of losing a $1,000 bet.

Anyway, I won't forget it. I thought it was wonderful, a great day to remember.

Chapter Fourteen

The Ghost Fleet of Mallows Bay

By Cap'n Larry Jarboe

Did you know that the largest concentration of sunken ships in the Western Hemisphere lies in the Potomac River just offshore of Charles County?

Over two hundred ships, mostly archaic wooden steamships from the WWI era, were scuttled and scrapped inside the shallow bay at Mallows Cove near Nanjemoy, Maryland, which also exists in another place and time.

Most of these ships originated as a grand government plan that turned into another boondoggle. To counter the devastation that the German U-boats were inflicting upon Allied shipping in World War I, the War Department per the recommendation of the U.S. Shipping Board contracted the construction of a monthly allotment of 200,000 tons of wooden steamships. Even in 1917, wooden steamboats were a thing of the past, but they were easier to build than steel ships, and wood was in plentiful supply.

When the war ended on November 11, 1919, not a single wooden steamship contracted by the Shipping Board had motored into a European port. By 1922, the Emergency Fleet Corporation offered all 226 for sale as one unit. The greatest portion of the fleet was sold for a total of three-quarter million dollars, which was about a half percent of the original cost.

The initial scrapping operation at the shipyard in Alexandria turned sour when the first two nearly 300 foot long vessels to be scrapped caught fire and delayed work at the shipyard for four months.

Ultimately, the "wooden navy" ended up in the desolate shallow Mallows Cove far up the Potomac on the Maryland side. There the Widewater Marine and Salvage Company of Alexandria, Virginia, set up a massive scrapping operation across from the Quantico U.S. Marine Base much to the chagrin of our local Maryland fishermen.

Then, the Depression hit. Scrap metal prices plummeted. WM&SC went belly up, and local scrappers took up residence at Mallows Bay, eking out a living by pulling metal from the timbers of those derelict steamers.

Today, many of these ships and other vessels as well lie on the shallow Potomac bottom. Dozens of hulls protrude above the water. Low tide at Mallows Bay provides an eerie view of the past as ship ribs, and iron spikes jut above the surface of the Potomac River.

Now, these wrecks provide habitat for fish and are also becoming the foundation for strangely shaped islands as trapped silt becomes soil for trees to take root in.

In 2010, Charles County Government and the Maryland Department of Natural Resources built a beautiful boat ramp and separate canoe/kayak launch where a large maritime scrap yard once operated. Fishermen can catch a wide variety of fresh and saltwater fish from the surrounding waters. Largemouth Bass, Bluegill, Channel and Blue Catfish, White and Yellow Perch, Norfolk Spot, Crappie, Striped Bass, and Northern Snakeheads may be caught in the shallow bay and quiet cove adjacent to the shore. Bald Eagles, Blue Herons, ospreys, ducks, and many other birds may be observed in the air and on the water.

The Mallows Bay Public Launch is twenty miles west of LaPlata, Maryland. From Rt. 301 take Route 6 West and turn right on Rt. 344. In a couple miles, turn left on Rt. 224. Four miles later, turn right on Wilson Landing Road. Better yet, check it out on MapQuest.

Mallows Bay Park is one of the most unique places to visit in all of Southern Maryland. The gates open at 5:30 AM and close at dusk. There is no fee to come in to sightsee, fish, or launch your boat. With savings like that, you can afford to pick up a copy of Don Shomette's Book, "Ghost Fleet of Mallows Bay," to get the whole story about this very intriguing infamous place that so few of us know about.

The largest ghost fleet in North America. *Photos by Cap'n Larry Jarboe*

Chapter Fifteen

The Country Philosopher - Stephen Gore Uhler

The Country Philosopher

Massive Cat Slaughter Might Be Next

By Stephen Gore Uhler
(I know, I didn't quit writing after all)

George Orwell, in his novel "1984", foretold the coming of an egalitarian society that would be so equal, yet some people would be "more equal than others."

This time has come.

Our school board has passed an edict that forbids peanuts of any kind in the diet of County school children. No peanut butter, no peanut bars, peanut dust. Not a molecule of the lovely peanut.

Why?

Because there is a child somewhere in the County, who has a super allergy to peanuts. So sensitive is this child that even a whiff of peanut aroma could be fatal.

Our hearts go out to that child and his parents, his allergy must be a constant worry for them. But, is that justification for radically altering the diet of the other 99.99 % of children not similarly affected.

What's next?

Are they going to disallow ham and pork chops because a Muslim child might be offended, suppose there was a P.E.T.A. child in the school? They would have to bar animal products or any sort?

And suppose we had a "bubble boy" (the child who lacks any immune system at all and has to be raised in a sterile bubble). Would we then require the other children not to breathe?

Peanuts are a staple part of our diet added to many of our prepared foods that the parents of a peanut sensitive child must have their hands full to keep their child uncontaminated, but, does that justify imposing hardship on parents of the great percentage who are not affected.

I am sensitive to poison ivy. Why has the county not come up with a multimillion-dollar scheme to rid the county of that noxious plant?

I have a neighbor who is allergic to cats. Why not a massive cat slaughter throughout the County.

The lowly peanut has been the mainstay of poor people for generations. Being a child of the Great Depression, schooled during the deprived years of WWII, I got to know peanut butter up close and personal. I carried peanut butter sandwiches five days a week, as did every other kid in the class.

The rich kids made their sandwiches palatable by slathering generous layers of Concord grape jelly. We poor kids used molasses for the same purpose.

Kids nowadays probably don't know what I mean by unpalatable peanut butter. The brands now all compete to be more smooth and creamy.

But Lord help us, back in the "good old days," peanut butter was packed in jars like cement mortar. You had to chisel it out of the jar.

And don't try to hold a conversation with your tablemates back in the "good old days" as that old-time peanut better clove to the roof of your mouth for hours. Cold milk only made it stick harder. If you were fortunate enough to have hot cocoa, you could melt it loose in half the time.

I read a scientific study last week in the Washington Post, which proved a theory that I have maintained for years that children nowadays are raised too delicately.

The study wanted to find out why the immune systems of modern-day kids were just not working. All sorts of new allergies, asthma, hives, digestive problems were showing up that could not be explained.

In the controlled study, they found the answer. Children who were exposed in infancy to all sorts of bacteria in primitive surroundings were free of allergies, while the rate of allergy in children "properly raised" under the most modern hygienic conditions were showing increasing rates of allergy.

You never heard of sickly, asthmatic children back in the "good old days" when we grew up running through cow yards and hog pens; when we didn't have electricity, no refrigeration or air conditioning, no indoor plumbing, our bathing was a Saturday ritual in the old #2 galvanized tub.

I found out how tough my immune system was after I left the farm and joined the U.S.A.F.

There came a time when the group I was assigned to had finished a particular school and should have moved routinely into the next phase.

But alas, the Air Force had made a scheduling boo-boo and had no school available for six weeks.

We sat around and sat around, young and full of vinegar, we wanted to get on with our studies. Finally, an officer came up with an idea. We were allowed to enroll as guinea pigs for some aerospace studies that were just beginning at that time.

Now you talk about fun!

The scientist hooked us up to wires, then accelerated our bodies, decelerated us; they compressed and decompressed us. First, we were weightless, and then we weighed a ton. They put a hurting on our tough young bodies, but it was exciting.

Then came an experiment to test exotic food poisons. The doctor in charge told us straight upfront that we would become violently ill, and anyone who didn't want to go any further could opt-out at that time. We were brave young men, didn't really give a damn, and figuring it was our patriotic duty, signed up.

"Men, you are going to get sick in a hurry, but not to worry, we will be right here with the antidote." We all drank doses of the toxic brew and shortly 19 out of 20 were retching and puking, I alone was unaffected by the mysterious concoction.

"Hmm," said the head doctor, "you must have immunity against this particular strain, we will try another on you."

And nothing.

Finally, the old doctor went back to a locked safe and came out with botulism that would kill any organism on the planet. He told his aides, "Watch this subject closely. In an hour's time, he will be violently ill."

Well, the hour went by, another hour, and another.

"Son," the kindly old doctor said, "You are dismissed from this experiment, your immune system blocks out everything we try. I don't understand it. Where did you grow up?"

I told him my history: raised on a tobacco farm in St. Mary's County, Maryland, playing in cow yards and hog pens, eating unrefrigerated food, and of course, proudly boasted of getting a bath every Saturday night in the old No. 2 tub.

The doctor was busy scribbling in the journal, "Tell me, you said you had no refrigeration, how did you keep the milk from the cows you had?"

We just set the milk out in open bowls until it became clabber and ate the clabber. My immune system must have greatly impressed the learned doctor because a few months later, clabber was on the line in all Air Force chow halls, only they called it yogurt.

***

"There is no finer investment for any community than putting milk into babies." – Winston Churchill 1874-1965

***

Steve Uhler with a lamb. *THE CHESAPEAKE photo*

Chapter Sixteen

Prize snakehead fish on display at Buzz's Marina, Ridge, Md.

Fish Tips

Snakehead Capture and Control

By Cap' Larry Jarboe

On my first exploration of Mallows Bay, I was honored to meet a master angler and archer named James Berry. That August day, James had four Northern Snakehead fish in his cooler that he had shot while bow fishing. If you do a Google search of [James Berry snakehead], you will discover his YouTube videos documenting his archery skills. James is one of a growing number of archers targeting this invasive species that threatens to damage the catch and release bass fishery that has become established on the Potomac River.

James provided me with an extensive education of snakehead habits. He has turned many tags back to the Maryland Department of Natural Resources from snakeheads that he has killed to help them track the movements of this predatory species. He also fillets, eats, and shares his fish to educate people on the excellent flavor of Chesapeake Snappers (a.k.a. snakeheads).

James has twice witnessed snakehead fish lifting their heads out of the water to spot a bug on a lily pad and then bump the plant to knock the insect into the water where it was slurped down. Mike Henderson at Buzz's Marina has observed a Northern Snakehead driving Bull Minnows (killifish) out of the water and then easing its head onto the shore to eat the flopping fish.

We are dealing with a very smart fish from Asia.

James Berry has watched snakeheads torpedo up behind a plastic frog lure then raise their pectoral fins in a quick stop. They are smart enough to know an imitation from the real thing.

Snakeheads also will take off when an archer draws his or her bow. They can see the movement from below and have figured out that they are not the top predator in this particular food chain. Again, we are dealing with a very smart fish.

Presently, the thick Hydrilla weed along the Potomac shore is helping water quality but providing much cover for snakeheads to hide in.

Probably, the best time to harvest and kill these fish is during the springtime nesting season. Despite their notorious reputation, Northern Snakeheads are good parents. They pair off to lay and fertilize eggs. Both parent fish hover nearby the school of fish fry to protect their progeny from predation from other fish. Though snakeheads are vicious predators, their babies are candy for other fish. Mother Nature does indeed have a sense of humor.

If snakeheads are targeted during the time when the larger snakeheads are protecting their fry, there are advantages: The water is usually clear since the algal growth is down. Fish are more in the open as the Hydrilla has not grown up. And, the parent fish are less likely to leave their offspring to hide. After killing the mated pair with bow and arrow, the fry ball is easy pickings for other fish to feed upon. Ironically, bow fishermen/women and the voracious little Mosquito fish (Gambusia) may be our best means of controlling this species, which we will never eradicate.

Added to this irony is the fact that the Maryland legislature had made the most specialized, efficient means of snakehead control illegal in Maryland. Though fishing with bow and arrow for snakeheads was specified as legal in the COMAR (Code of Maryland), crossbows were not allowed to harvest snakeheads. DNR, with a little urging by me, changed this regulation. Hats off to DNR!

This means that you can now legally use an efficient, easy to aim crossbow to target this alien predator in the State of Maryland.

Meanwhile, the General Assembly has enacted legislation targeting your toilet. But that is another story!

Larry Jarboe - bass21292@yahoo.com

***

"Women are tricks of slight of hand, which, to admire, we should not understand." – William Congreve 1670-1729
***

Todd Murphy of Marbury, Md. with Maryland record snakehead.

Chapter Seventeen

Cardinal James Hickey with a newly confirmed Catholic at Immaculate Heart of Mary Church in Lexington Park, Md.
photo by Ken Rossignol

Just Call Me Cardinal

By Ken Rossignol

It was Sunday morning, and a great honor was soon to happen to the parish at Immaculate Heart of Mary Church in Lexington Park, Maryland. James Cardinal Hickey was to celebrate Mass and perform the Sacrament of Confirmation to a large group of young and old.

On the way to the church, I suddenly became preoccupied with thoughts, different from my usual ones, on the way to the church. Gone was the preoccupation with what pocket did I have the lifesavers in and did I remember some money for the collection. Protocol. What a strange word for someone connected with *The Chesapeake.*

Here we are the epitome of a relaxed attitude, and I am worried about the correct order of things. In particular, I am concerned if Darrin Farrell, our ace photographer, is allowed to use his flash in the church or if such flashing should be saved till Mass is over. As I was early for the event, I stopped by the rectory and knocked on the back door. In a short moment, an older priest, who I assumed must be an aide to the Cardinal, answered the door. He started to open the door, and it was sticking at the bottom. He tugged and pulled as hard as he could, all to no avail. Seeing that he seemed like my presence at the door was not an intrusion, and he would like to help me, I gave the door a healthy, well-placed kick at the bottom, as the priest pulled again. Wham! The door flew open, and the priest fell backward onto the floor. I helped him up as he laughed.

I inquired of Father Mike Wilson's presence, and the old priest told me Father Mike had already gone to the church. Sensing that Father Mike would be involved in preparing for Mass, I decided to ask the advice of the visiting priest. He replied that he didn't know what Father Mike's policy was on the matter. I then asked the priest what he thought I should do. He replied that perhaps the best thing to do was to wait until Mass was over before taking photos. I told him that I agreed and would do so and thanked him for his help. I then went on to church to join my family, who I thought was already there. As the congregation rose for the procession leading the Cardinal in the church, I turned and just a few feet away from me, robed in the vestments of a Prince of the Catholic Church, walking with his symbolic shepherd's staff, was the older priest from the rectory. He looked over at me and seeing the expression on my face, just smiled and winked

After Mass was over, and photographs were taken (I took them as Darrin overslept), the last person to pose for their picture with the Cardinal left the altar, and I was left with the Cardinal again. We talked of his love for the area that the Archdiocese of Washington covered and of Ohio where spent time as a Bishop and of his home state of Michigan. Since I had used the term "Father" when addressing him before Mass, and I now knew that was probably not appropriate any longer, I inquired as to whether I should call him "Father" or "Your Eminence." He thought for a second and said, "Just call me Cardinal."

All in all, meeting the Cardinal was good for the sinner. He was an articulate man who gave a challenging sermon during the Mass that day, and you could feel the joy of those receiving confirmation as full members of their church.

As for myself, I suppose I should go to the front doors of rectories in the future and stop asking dumb questions. And be very careful in the future to not knock a Prince of the Church on his can.

Chapter Eighteen

Lenny's Latest Serving

Peace an' Quiet an' Fishin'

By Lenny Rudow

One of the greatest things about fishin' is the peace an' quiet in the outdoors, away from the stress and noise of civilization.

Of course, sometimes people have trouble finding that fishin' hole where ya can be alone and still catch fish. If you've been through the frustration of arriving at your local spot to find a crowd of people breakin' the peace an' quiet, I've got some tips for you.

It took me years to develop a system to keep the litterers and noise-makers away, but I think I've finally got it perfected. Here's how ya do it:

1. In preparation for any trip, when you go to the bait shop, be sure to whisper about the great fishin' up the road – in the opposite direction of where you're goin'! (Careful, this can backfire if you mention a place with possibilities and people really do get lots of fish.)
2. If you're fishin' in a crowded location, let some feller overhear ya talkin' about the dangerous chemical leak that took place upstream last week.
3. Tell people you're working for the DNR, catching samples to see if people really do get sick from the fish here.
4. If these methods fail and there is still a crowd, after making sure no one you know is there, chant in Latin, make bug-eyes, and play with your bait knife.

If' n' these methods don't work, the crowd persists, and you can't get any fish, you can still redeem your fisherman's honor in several ways.

1. Know the location and closing time of the nearest seafood market on the way home from your fishing hole.
2. Use a bait ya can serve for dinner if skunked – crawfish work good for this as Minnies make great sushi. If you used worms, forget this advice.
3. Claim that every huge fish you caught (and there were lots of 'em) had a closed season.
   Remember, if none of these work, you can call up the TV

station and tell 'em about the big one that got away. They love it when you can email them a photo. Be sure to use one from last year.

Lenny Rudow with a King Mackerel.

Chapter Nineteen

The Amish Way

By Amos Arthur Holmes

I have always admired the Amish way of life. These gentle people, who combine hard work with common sense, have become almost perfect in the art of farming.

But, are they really as great as people say they are? Is their tobacco the best? Is their livestock superior? Can they get more out of an acre of land than anybody else?

I decided to find out. I'm not a farmer. I'm a writer and a lover. But could I, without any experience, live like the Amish, do and become a better farmer than any of them?

Will, I decided to give it a try.

I bought myself a twenty-acre farm up near Mechanicsville. The farmhouse was built in 1910 and was in desperate need of repair. There was a huge hole in the roof, and the doors hung haphazardly from their hinges.

On my first day at the farm, I was contemplating the vast amount of work ahead of me when my wife, JoLoyce, came up and said: "Amos, there is an Amish man outside who wants to see you."

"Ah! I said, "That's Mr. Stoltzfus. He has come to sell me a horse and buggy."

I went outside and paid for the horse and buggy. The old Amish gentleman left, and I stood looking at my purchase.

"I didn't know you could handle horses," said JoLoyce.

"Of course I can handle horses. Nothing to it. Here, let me show you."

I took a seat in the buggy, grasped the reins, and shouted, "Giddyup."

Nothing happened

"Giddyup," I screamed.

Nothing.

"Amos," said JoLoyce, "maybe the horse only understands German."

"That's a thought. What is the German word for giddyup?"

"I think it's Auf Wiedersehen."

"AUF WIEDERSEHEN," I bellowed.

The horse didn't move.

JoLoyce went in to inspect the house, and I got down from the buggy. I stood wondering if I would have to teach that horse English before I could get him to move.

I went up to the barn to see my cow. She was a pretty thing, all brown with white spots, and as I stood admiring her, she went to the bathroom. Now when a cow goes to the bathroom, she goes to the bathroom. I'm talking about production. I was horrified. I couldn't have my animals running around messing up my barn. How in the devil do you potty-train a cow? Ah! I would use diapers. JoLoyce walked into the barn. Her face was ashen. "Amos," she cried, "there's no bathroom in our house."

I handed her an empty sardine can.

"What's this?"

"You said you had to go to the bathroom."

"When you die," said JoLoyce, "I want them to perform an autopsy just to see if you really have gone through this life without a brain."

I took JoLoyce's hand. Inhaling with great gusto, I sighed, "Just smell that air."

"Smells like cow manure," replied JoLoyce.

"Look," I snapped, "Don't be so negative. How can I be a better farmer than the Amish if you aren't a better wife than an Amish wife? I want you to do four quilts a day, learn how to use that wood stove, make shoofly pie every ten minutes, and stop whining about something as unnecessary as a bathroom."

JoLoyce went off in a huff (I noticed that she took the sardine can), and I stood thinking about my first day as a farmer. Not too bad, really. I would have to teach that horse English and get the diaper on the cow, but things were looking up. Tomorrow I'll hitch JoLoyce to the plow and plant ten acres in cantaloupes. The Amish say I can't grow cantaloupes in the winter. But what do they know? Now, if you'll excuse me, I've got to go milk the bull.

Chapter Twenty

Ben Bradlee selected for Medal of Freedom

By Ken Rossignol

ST. MARY'S CITY --- It isn't often that a resident of St. Mary's County (even a weekend resident) is selected for one of the 500 Medal of Freedom awards that have been given out by U. S. presidents over the last fifty years, but Drayden resident Ben Bradlee now joins that group.

President Obama announced recently the honor for Bradlee, the tough editor of the Washington Post, who kept his junior reporters on a story about the burglary of the Democratic National Committee headquarters that ultimately led to the resignation of President Richard Nixon.

Obama's recognition of Bradlee is about as close as any president has wanted to get to Bradlee since 1974, as such a photo op might inspire future investigative journalists to emulate Bob Woodward, Carl Bernstein, and Bradlee himself. It was suggested to Bill Clinton that he put Bradlee up for the award, and according to the Washington Post, Clinton referring to Bradlee's wife, Sally Quinn, uttered: anyone who sleeps with that b----- deserves a medal." Clinton, who was impeached but not convicted by the

Senate, failed to give Bradlee the award but will stand next to him this year as a fellow recipient.

Famed Watergate Editor as Coach for GOP Officials

That sounds odd, doesn't it?

At lunch in Trader Vic's in Washington DC in 1995, hosted by Bradlee for the purpose of giving his view on government to two newly elected Republican St. Mary's County Commissioners, Larry Jarboe, and Chris Brugman, Bradlee had a lot to say about the GOP takeover of Congress in the previous year's election.

One thing that he said that stood out in my mind was that with so many Republicans elected to Congress that year (1994) and the dramatic shift of GOP being in charge of Congress for the first time in forty years, that there would be plenty for reporters to write about.

"They will be able to come to work and fill their lunch buckets every day," Bradlee said.

Bradlee had consented to the meeting with the newly elected GOP county commissioners at my request to take part in a group which would act as an orientation for Jarboe and Brugman, to counter that being prepared by the defeated 'Good Old Boys' then-St. Mary's County Administrator, Ed Cox.

Jarboe and Brugman, along with fellow Republicans Paul Chesser, Barbara Thompson and Frances Eagan, had made a clean sweep of the St. Mary's Commissioner board in the election in 1994, a historic realignment which has resulted in the board continuing to be held by a majority of Republicans with the exception of the four-year period from 1998 to 2002 when only Republican Shelby Guazzo served.

End of Bradlee Era at Historic St. Mary's City

Former St. Mary's City Commission Chairman Ben Bradlee said in 2004 that the new appointments by Governor Robert Ehrlich to the Historic St. Mary's Commission were excellent choices and a great boost to the goal of blending preservation of Maryland's history and promoting the enjoyment of the site by the public.

Gov. Ehrlich, in 2004, made a round of recess appointments to the outdoor museum devoted to preserving and explaining the history of Maryland's colonial capital located on the banks of the St. Mary's River at St. Mary's City.

Along with the selection of new appointees to the came the choice by the commission of a new chairman to succeed the long-time chairman, Ben Bradlee.

"Dick Moe was chairman of the National Trust for Historic Preservation for ten years and is a top-notch choice to lead the commission," said Bradlee at the time of the changeover. Bradlee was selected to be chairman of the St. Mary's City Commission by former Governor William Donald Schaefer in 1991.

Bradlee was asked if he was able to survive the rough and tumble of local St. Mary's politics after only being prepared by the amateur antics of the nation's capital.

"This was tough at first, but we worked with a great group of folks over the years, we were able to get the consolidation with the college five years ago and that was a real plus, now we have a great director, a really top-notch guy with Dick Moe as chairman and I am glad to be able to stick around to work with them all," said Bradlee in an interview in 2004 at his home at Portobello.

"We have a great group of fascinating people who really believe in the purpose of preserving the history of Maryland at this site, and they have a lot of ability, they are just a great group, and I am really happy to see the appointments made by the Governor, it just makes a lot of sense," Bradlee told me in the interview for ST. MARY'S TODAY.

Bradlee, who has been the longest-serving chairman since the commission was formed, remained on the commission and on the St. Mary's College Board of Trustees until finally ending his service in recent years.

More progress at showing the taxpayers something for their money invested in the historic site was made during Bradlee's tenure as chairman than at any time since the original land purchases were made to assemble and preserve the colonial capital.

During Bradlee's 13-year stint at the helm of the commission, the man who became the most famous newspaper editor in America at his job as executive editor of the Washington Post oversaw an ambitious series of projects to turn around the lackluster colonial capital.

Putting St. Mary's City 'On the Map'

Most weeks, St. Mary's City had more people underground at the Trinity Church cemetery than tourists above-ground viewing exhibits or scenery.

Bradlee vowed to 'put this place on the map,' an expression which Bradlee has often used to describe the impact of the Post coverage of the Watergate scandal, which resulted in the resignation of President Richard M. Nixon and put the Post 'on the map.'

During Bradlee's first year on the job, a part-time devotion he mixed in with his duties as a full-time vice president at the Post, he launched the now famous Lead Coffins Project.

Bradlee also convinced Gov. Schaefer to fund $500,000 to move the huge old country 1840-era manor house from where it was built in the middle of the old capital city several miles away to a riverfront site off of Rosecroft Road where it was then turned into a bed and breakfast inn with facilities for dining and receptions.

After years of trying, the Broome-Howard Inn closed its doors, and Lisa and Michael Kelly now operate the Ruddy Duck at Solomon's Island and have recently taken over the old Evans Crabhouse when Old Line Bank ended up with the property following a controversial bank scheme. The story of what happened at the St. George Island hotel and restaurant, now run by the Kelly's and formerly owned by Chuck Kimball, is told in the *Bank of Crooks & Criminals,* available on Amazon in paperback and eBook.

Bradlee, even though he was the chairman of the St. Mary's City Commission and responsible for overseeing the operations of the commission, stuck his neck out financially to try to see to it that the restaurant and catering operations would make a go of it. The facility was desperately needed at the time, to assist the college in its goals of becoming a world-class educational institution which had as its only eating facilities, the college snack bar, and the nearby Green Door, a redneck bar a few miles from the campus.

Assisted Young Couple to Get Business Loan

To see to it that the Kelly's got the loan that they needed to be able to buy the equipment and fund their startup in the old house which was moved to the field overlooking the St. Mary's River, Bradlee told me he co-signed the loan at Maryland Bank & Trust.

Bradlee's co-signing the loan for the operator of the restaurant where the College and Historic St. Mary's City held lavish receptions for years might well be unorthodox and perhaps illegal, but it was done solely for the intent to help a young couple make a go off it and at great financial risk to Bradlee. Since the restaurant failed, it could well be that Bradlee ended up paying the balance of the loan, if any.

Most of those who seek appointments to the clubby boards of St. Mary's College and Historic St. Mary's City are usually out to build their resumes and suck up to the wealthy and powerful.

When Bradlee was appointed to head Historic St. Mary's City, I warned him that the locals would chew him up and spit him out. He laughed and said he was used to it. As it all turned out, it appeared he held his own.

At a meeting in his office with ST. MARY'S TODAY reporter John C. Wright, to discuss the looming underground digs at the colonial capital, the hard-charging reporter for my newspaper asked Bradlee a series of probing questions.

Bradlee looked at Wright, and said, "hold it, fella, I have been doing this since before you were born...", I interrupted the two and reminded Wright that we were here only to do a report on the lead coffins, and he could save his energy for the St. Mary's County Commissioners and the Good Old Boys back home.

Later reporting in the paper earned a couple of strongly worded letters from Bradlee about subsequent critical coverage of his efforts at St. Mary's City, but he kept up his subscription until I sold the newspaper in 2010, and we remained on friendly terms. It is quite the privilege to be chewed out by America's most famous editor.

Ben Bradlee, right, was tapped by Maryland Governor William Donald Schaefer, left, holding a Lead Coffins t-shirt, to be Chairman of the Historic St. Mary's City Commission. Director Burt Kummerow is at the center on the day of the reveal. *Photo by Ken Rossignol*

Much Ado about Stale Air in Lead Coffins

The lead coffins excavation in Chapel Field, the site of the first Catholic Brick Chapel in the original 13 colonies, was an ambitious project to determine the identity of those persons entombed in lead coffins discovered under the unexplored substructure of the first brick Catholic chapel at St. Mary's City.

Bradlee's efforts resulted in unprecedented numbers of visitors and media streaming to St. Mary's City from around the world to watch the progress of the exploration.

Television satellite trucks jammed the field near large Army tents, which were set up to provide shelter from the elements as the investigation reached a dramatic step when the coffins were finally disinterred.

With a press pool of national media peering over the shoulders of scientists, archaeologists, and anthropologists, the unusual lead coffins were carefully opened to reveal their human remains and tell the story of colonial life in Maryland, which had been sealed for more than 200 years.

Reporters filed news stories from the scene via cell phones, CNN covered the event, while ABC's Nightline sent its top reporter, Dave Maresh, and broadcast live at 11:30 p.m. from Chapel Field.

Nightline's anchor, Ted Koppel, a buddy of Bradlee's, lives in an old manor house around the bend, down-river from St. Mary's City, and was part of the magic Bradlee was able to set in motion to bring widespread notoriety, national stature and historic standing to Maryland's early beginnings.

Bradlee had set in motion a modern hi-tech version of a Barnum and Bailey Big Top atmosphere mixed with a historical Ripley's Believe or Not explanation of what they expected to learn and hoped to achieve from the examination of the lead coffins.

Benefits to modern times included speculation that scientists could learn about the relationships between colonial-era health and immune systems to solve modern health problems.

And just to keep up the more prurient interests of the public, Bradlee's troop of professors and scientists continued to suggest that the bones of the biggest coffin were likely that of Maryland's colonial governor, Phillip Calvert.

After the big dig, the coffins were shipped off to laboratories at the Smithsonian for more research, and it was later determined that the woman in a second lead coffin was likely

Calvert's second wife, proving that even then, most dead guys didn't get buried with their first wives when they remarried.

While teams of experts in pathology, insects, colonial-era vegetation, fabrics, disease, pollen, and bones were assembled to examine the coffins and their contents, the public was involved in every step of the process.

Groups came by bus to tour and to learn what an examination of "stale air" could provide modern society.

While some might call the lead coffins effort government-sponsored grave-robbing, others could say it was simply entertainment and thrills for geeks not able to review the work of professors breaking into Egyptian tombs.

The work of the Lead Coffins project led into the plans for the restoration of the Brick Chapel, which was built by Jesuits around 1667 and later ordered shuttered by order of the Protestant Governor of Maryland in 1705.

While the restoration and reconstruction of the brick chapel have been subject to false starts and a near-war over staff plans to simply use the chapel as a visitor's center, a new twist to the plans came about as a result of intervention by Senator Roy Dyson (D. St. Mary's, Calvert).

The historic commission authorized a probe into what the chapel looked like and assured the public that the extensive research would result in an authentic recreation of the chapel, and it would not be subject to any inappropriate activities.

The chapel site still has about 300 people buried under and near the chapel, posing special problems for the construction effort, which is not allowed to disturb any of the burial sites to install utilities. The site remains a protected cemetery under state law and is a consecrated Catholic cemetery in spite of the removal of the chapel due to the order outlawing the open worshiping by Catholics as religious intolerance became the law of the land in Maryland, a condition which existed up until the American Revolution.

The chapel research into the construction techniques of the era reveals that the church was likely 22 to 25 feet tall, and the foundation shows that it was built in the shape of a cross.

St. Mary's City has been the battleground for some volunteers who believe that they know best how to run things with many elitists taking action to rid the outdoor museum of the volunteers that they could not control and replace them with paid staff.

Bradlee set into motion a plan to consolidate Historic St. Mary's City under the St. Mary's College, two groups who had battled each other in turf wars for years.

Initially opposed by Sen. Dyson, the plan to marry the two panels finally won approval after assurances were made that the College would not decimate the commission.

Bradlee argued that it made sense for the College and Commission to share staff, expenses, and work together to preserve the same small village that they both occupy.

The College finally began taking a major step as Bradlee ended his era, towards making the St. Mary's River a laboratory for environmental sciences with a new waterfront facility located at the boathouse area of the college.

Maggie's Erection

That effort turned into a major issue in 2008 when the college erected a huge three-story new boathouse, which changed the very vista of the area, which, ironically, was part of the mission that Historic St. Mary's City Commission was charged with protecting. Also, the construction work was done in violation of Maryland soil erosion and pollution laws, which, if done by an individual or business, could have resulted in fines and imprisonment.

Vows to set fire to the boathouse were reported in ST. MARY'S TODAY, along with the admonition that arson is never a good idea and soon St. Mary's College President Maggie O'Brien was calling in fire marshals, erecting 10-foot high construction fences and facing down an enraged community, all of which finally led to her resignation. But the boathouse was built as a lasting monument to bureaucratic and elitist superiority over the community.

The previous major use the College made of the river, besides for the sailing team, was to use it as a sewage discharge point. That problem was finally corrected with a sewage line connecting the college with the county's sewage treatment plant, which serves Lexington Park.

Citizens who were active in saving St. Mary's City from being overrun by the College pointed out various construction projects which unearthed Indian village remains and paved over early settler's homes without any archeological digs performed.

The new commission/college alliance guided by Bradlee was aimed at preventing such events from occurring again and from fostering a new spirit of cooperation, which actually seems to have taken place – while he was there, but that quickly ended, as shown by the Boathouse fiasco.

But regardless of the viewpoints of those who enjoy St. Mary's City and believe it important, Bradlee has been a key figure in the long-term success of the colonial capital museum.

At the age of eighty-four when he ended his service at St. Mary's City, Bradlee remained a vigorous Washington Post executive and had his hand in a number of projects for the huge conglomerate around the world and with local concerns in St. Mary's City, where he maintains a weekend home to escape Washington.

"With Marty Sullivan as the director, this place has really improved, and we have ironed out problems which we inherited," said Bradlee. "This is a great way to involve students in learning about history and taking part in discovering colonial life and our early beginnings. It is exciting to be a part of this and to work with such a great group of people."

Sullivan did stick around for some years before moving on to other employment.

At the age of ninety, when setting up a day to meet Ben for lunch, which had become a fairly regular event since Bradlee began subscribing to my newspaper, he told me: "just pick a day, my calendar is empty, no one wants to talk to a ninety-year-old guy."

When I met him at his office on 15th Street, I told him we could take my truck over to the Jefferson Hotel for lunch. "No problem, its only three blocks, we'll walk."

That could well be why he is now ninety-one, and he does have one more thing to add to his calendar, a meeting at the White House to pick up his award.

At lunch, as always, he refused to let me pick up the check, and when he tried to pay with his credit card, the waiter came back and told him that his card was declined. While the Post was experiencing the dire consequences of the great decline in revenue, it was more likely his card had expired. I tried to pay, and he refused, then he ordered the waiter to call the manager, whom Bradlee told to "just keep the damn bill here, and I'll pay it the next time I come in." The manager quickly agreed.

Bradlee, a close pal of President John F. Kennedy, while traveling in high-society and as the executive editor of the Washington Post guided the now-sold newspaper through a path of prestigious Pulitzer's, had two things on his resume that always impressed me as showing that he was cut from the same cloth as the rest of us. Bradlee served as executive officer on a U. S. Navy destroyer for several years during the height of World War II in the South Pacific, and after the war, he spent a stint helping to run a weekly newspaper in New Hampshire.

Bradlee and millions of other veterans put their lives on the line to protect our freedoms and then worked hard to print the news that the powerful never wanted to be told. While it didn't work out too well in New Hampshire, he scored a big fish in Washington, and we all owe him his Medal of Freedom. He earned it.

For myself, I will always remember Bradlee, not only for the incidents above but for getting the *Washington Post* to do a serious take on what their cutesy reporter Annie Gowen had branded the "paper caper." When Sheriff Richard Voorhaar, states attorney candidate Richard Fritz and six deputies set out on election eve to seize control of all available copies of ST. MARY'S TODAY, the result was that voters could not read critical articles of these candidates before voting.

Bradlee decided that the Washington Post would weigh into the story when we met for lunch at the hotel across the street from his office. He called Post Vice President Carol Melamed to meet with me, and soon, the Post began to change its coverage to serious, with a front-page story appearing several months later, which led to my being invited to tell the story of how the cops cleaned out my newsstands on Good Morning America. Many follow-up articles by Eugene L. Meyer and other Post reporters took a serious take on the newspaper raid and the resulting court decisions.

WUSA reporter Bruce Leshan did a story on the actions of Fritz as well as the story of him pleading guilty to rape, along with two other men. Fritz did plead guilty, according to court records, but in an interview with Chris Wallace on ABC 20/20, Fritz said the sex was consensual, which the victim denied and said was forcible rape.

The WUSA article won the news organization an Emmy while Fritz's answer to Wallace, now the host of *Fox News Sunday* when asked if he expected people to believe that a 15-year-old girl would willingly have sex with three young men, he answered: "it happens all the time."

Following years of litigation, the Fourth Circuit United States Court of Appeals ruled that the acts of Fritz, Voorhaar, and the deputies violated the Constitutional rights of myself and my readers and ordered the lower court to reverse it's earlier ruling and proceed to trial. The defendants soon settled the case, and the published opinion of the court is now the law of the land; see Rossignol v Voorhaar. The complete story is told in the book, *The Story of The Rag*, available in paperback and eBook on Amazon.

Bradlee told me after the Court of Appeals ruling that his Washington Post lawyers had said the ruling was the most significant in forty years – since his win on the Pentagon papers.

Therefore, I am really happy that Bradlee has been awarded the Medal of Freedom. He did a good job for America and far more to help protect our First Amendment rights in St. Mary's County than most retirees.

Chapter Twenty One

Of Men's & Hens

By Tony Marconi

It was one of those parties. You know. Not the kind where everyone goes with their husbands or wives and has a few drinks while making small talk about their jobs and the kids. The other kind. Where a hostess invites just the women and serves them all soft drinks and coffee cake so one of her friends can show off the latest merchandise, the Corporation has come up with.

I'd never been to one before, but I certainly had an opinion about them. Last refuge for the bored housewife. Nothing better to do than sit around and gossip and spend good money on a bunch of dust-catching knick-knacks. Or more rubber bowls. Or five pounds of plaster and body paint – uh, cosmetics. It'd be a cold day south of the border before you'd catch me getting suckered into wasting an evening like that.

Besides, I was a man, and men, house-husbands or not, are generally left off the invitation lists when these bashes are put together. So, I figured I'd never be faced with telling a neighbor thanks, but no thanks.

Until last month.

I'd had one of those days with the kids. The kind where you wonder why you'd let them live until supper because you're going to kill them afterward anyway. My wife had just gotten home when our good friend, Cindy, ran over to drop off some mis-delivered mail.

"Gotta' run," she said, "I'm late for a party."

My ears pricked up. I envisioned a few cold beers and some adult conversation.

"Party in the middle of the week, huh? What's the occasion?"

"No," she shook her head as if to indicate that I'd gotten it wrong.

"A Doodle-Daddle products party want to come?"

I knew she meant it as a joke, but her question coincided perfectly with a screech as my son pulled my daughter's hair. I looked at my wife.

"Would you mind?"

"Be my guest. You look like you need a break."

So I went. Though not without a few misgivings.

What, for instance, was I going to talk about with the soap-opera set? I didn't feel up to swapping recipes or exchanging helpful hints about how to remove mineral stains from bathroom tiles. Maybe one or two of them watched football, but they probably wouldn't know a tight end from a running back. And did any of them read? Something other than romance novels that is.

Oh, well. No one had twisted my arm to make me come. Better to just sit quietly and nod politely when I'm offered milk and cookies.

Cindy parked in front of a townhouse, and I followed her up the front steps.

The door swung open a moment later, the sounds of easy rock music and animated discussion spilling out to greet us. An attractive blonde lady in a stylish print dress smiled as she signaled us in.

"Hi, I'm Beth. Jennifer's sister. Make yourselves at home and have a drink. Wine and beer are in the fridge. There's some rum on the counter if you want to mix it with some coke."

I was led into the living room where a dozen well-dress ladies were sipping beverages and nibbling at plates full of cut veggies. Cindy introduced me around, and I immediately forget everyone's name. Someone handed me a Miller's Lite, and I sought the sanctuary of a chair in the corner.

A freckle-faced redhead in her mid-twenties turned to me.

"So what did you think about the 'Skins trading Schroeder?"

I was caught off guard. A football question?

"I hope they haven't made a mistake," she continued. "Williams is getting old for pro ball."

"But he's hardly over the hill," I finally recovered sufficiently to respond.

"True. And they've got plenty of time to bring Rypien along, don't they?"

The brunette sitting across from us turned and shook her head. "Trudy and the Redskins," she laughed. "I don't think Gibbs worries about them half as much as she does."

I smiled. "I take it you're not that big a fan?"

"Oh, to a certain degree, I am. But I'd rather spend my day unwinding with a good book."

"Gothic love stories?" I ventured a guess.

She looked at me like I was a cretin. "Who's got time for those, I'm into James Joyce."

"You read Joyce to relax?"

"Sure, I get tired of plowing through those environmental impact studies all week."

Trudy saw my expression of curiosity.

"Helen is a GS-16 with EPA," she explained.

"And what do you do?" I asked.

"I'm a lawyer for the House of Representatives."

"And you come to Doodle-Daddle parties after work?"

"Of course. It's a great way for all of us to get together."

"You all?"

"Uh-huh." She pointed around the room.

"Most of us were friends in school, but our jobs make it hard for us to stay touch these days."

"You mean, you're all working women?"

"But, of course. Kathy, over there, is a CPA. Diane is a cardiologist. Yvonne edits a newsletter. Cindy —"

"I know what Cindy does, she's the principal at my daughter's school."

"And what do you do, Tony?"

"I'm a house-husband," I said in a much too quiet voice.

"Really?" Helen sounded interested. "Do you do windows? I'm looking for good domestic help." She paused and gave me a suspicious look. "You don't spend a lot of time sitting on the couch watching soap operas, do you?"

My nasty reply was cut short by Beth's announcement that we would play a game. Fine with me. I thought about Helen's last remark and decided I was in a competitive mood. There seemed to be something more than a door prize at stake here though I wasn't sure just what.

Beth handed out paper and pencils and told us we'd collect points by answering questions. Ten points for wearing yellow, five for every piece of jewelry. Things like that.

By the fourth question, I knew I was lagging behind. Fifteen points for a red lipstick struck me as being a bit biased. I started to gain back some ground when they awarded twenty-five for kissing your mate that morning. Some of the women were single.

"How about if I got lucky last night?" Helen quipped. Or was it a boast?

We came down to the final stretch. Ten points for every button you were wearing. I had on a western-style shirt. With all those zippered dresses, no one came close.

Except for Helen. She had on a blouse, and it wasn't a pull-over.

I snuck a look at her total. She was thirty points ahead of me.

"What the heck," I thought. "It's a stupid game and a stupid party. I should've never come in the first place, see if you ever catch me at one these again."

"And now for the last question," Beth announced. "Add a hundred points if you're willing to host a Doodle-Daddle party in your home."

Everyone looked around and shook their heads. Even Helen put her pencil down.

"Not me, "I don't have the time. Besides, I think I've won."

I thought she gave me a look of triumph, but maybe it was just a reflection of light off her glasses.

The door prize, a porcelain chipmunk with over-sized eyes, is now displayed on my desk like a trophy. I think I may have felt more excited about winning it than the situation warranted. In fact, I'm almost sure of it. Especially when my friends start laughing whenever I invite them over to check it while they are viewing the rest of the product line.

Anyone interested in coming to a Doodle-Daddle Party?

***

"What I tell you three times is true." – Lewis Carroll

***

Chapter Twenty Two

Letter from High Chimneys

Seasoned by more than 22 years and flavored by the 12 years since his reassignment as Special Correspondent to The Heavenly Territories, Jack Rue's first column in The Chesapeake is presented once again.

I READ RUE! DO YOU?

By Jack Rue

It's How You Play the Game

Letter from High Chimneys
By Jack Rue

Helen Hayes said, "Life is just a walk around the block."

Her former home is on the Gold Coast at the Patuxent River Naval Air Station.

Benjamin Franklin said, "It's not about the amount of wealth one acquires but how you use it."

Mark Russell quipped, "Some Congressman have expressed alarm over new rules for Congress. They are alarmed, they asked if they have to spend all day being ethical, how can they do their jobs?"

This card from Manila reads: "Let me know how many write-in tombstone votes you need to take you over the top. I have hit pay dirt." Signed, President of your Far East Political Campaign, Kelly.

Kelly was going to Ypsilanti College at the same time as Fritz Duke and later became mayor of Wyandotte, Michigan. The Rue's had a reunion at the tavern we used to frequent before WWII. I took a walk down Main Street and had to relieve myself and used a telephone pole. This car with a light on top pulled up, and the back door opened, and this voice said, "Get in," which I did. I thought it was a taxi. I asked where we were going, and he replied, "to jail." I asked why. He said, "indecent exposure." I said, "You should congratulate me, not arrest me. You know my ancestors founded this town, and if you value your job, take me back to the bar". When we got there, another police car was there closing the place up as my older brother kept buying drinks and acting like a typical Rue!

Many moons ago, the Pale Brothers were stealing hogs from our farmers. Our Sheriff's Willard Long, Harry Lancaster, Bucky Redman, Bob Miedzinski, Joe Lee Somerville, Larry Williams, George Sanger, Don Purdy, Wayne Pettit (lots of votes here – I'm with Rue, how 'bout you?) had a conference and decided to catch them. One Sheriff car hid by the pen and the other by the gate. Sure enough, about dark here come the Pale Brothers, and they put a big hog in their car. When the Sheriff arrived, he asked the deputy guarding the gate where the Pale Brothers were. When the Pale Brothers returned to the gate with their stolen pig, they saw the lawmen and the blockade. They put a coat and hat on the pig and sat him in the backseat.

The Sheriff later told the story and claimed he shined a light on the driver and asked his name. Paul Pale, he replied. His brother replied, Pete Pale. "Then I shined the light on the back seat and that Oink Pale was the best looking of the Pale Brothers."

McGuilicudy and Mergatroid grew up, went to school together, graduated and took a job in the local brick factory, had a double wedding, and frequented Rue's Roost. One day, McGuilicudy came in alone, and I slid him his mug of beer down the bar. When I walked down to collect for the beer, I saw his face had stitches, iodine in cuts, an eyebrow missing, etc.

"What in the hell happened to you, and where in tarnation is Mergatroid?"

"I had a fight with my buddy."

"You mean a guy that small beat up on a guy as huge as you?"

"Yes, but you should have seen what he had in his hands."

"What did he have in his hands?"

"He had a spade, and he hit me right in the kisser."

"What did you have in your hands?"

"The best part of Mrs. Mergatroid, beautiful, but no good in a fight!"

My ancestors were missionaries, and the cannibal headhunters captured them. They put them in a big pot. When the water started boiling, my great-grandfather broke out in a smile. His brother asked what was funny. My great-grandfather replied, "I just seasoned their stew."

We had a friend that switched from Republican to Democrat to win an election. He used the "Good Old Boy" method, which was to slip a two-dollar bill and a miniature of liquor to each voter.

He had his political cronies file for Sheriff and gave them each $2,000 for campaign funds, figuring they would campaign for him. My recollection is that there were five or six of them that filed for Sheriff and had no intention of winning. One of his friends did not deliver the votes, and when he went to ask what happened, he found him on his farm, planting tobacco with a new John Deere tractor. My friend asked the erstwhile political operative what happened to the votes he thought he paid for. He replied, "I am riding on them."

Rue refused to let go of President Clinton's hand until he finished his joke.

Chapter Twenty Three

A Jumbo Shrimp Tale

By Cap'n Larry Jarboe

One of the most useful and least used baits in the Chesapeake watershed is the lowly grass shrimp. Though fishermen can get hundreds of these little critters for the small effort of pushing a fine mesh net through submerged shore grass, we often pay ten bucks for a dozen anemic bloodworms imported from New England.

Grass shrimp in our Bay and rivers grow not nearly so big as their southern cousins from North Carolina down through Florida. Still, our local fish love to bite on these small crustacean morsels.

Early summer is the time to catch more of the biggest grass shrimp that are loaded with eggs. These fat females are hardly an inch long, but they slide nicely on a #2 bait holder snelled hook. Later on, as the water warms, most of the grass shrimp caught will barely thread on a #4 hook.

This year, the grass shrimp have run larger later through summer than past seasons. If you push a grass shrimp roller net through the shore grass, you will have dozens of tasty little shrimp to cover the hook tip of the beetle spin lure that you should be casting for perch in the creeks this fall.

Quite a few years ago, I caught a nice mess of jumbo shrimp in a much bigger net.

Two friends of mine who were sports writers and photographers lived on a big farm on the Edisto River in South Carolina. While my wife, Carlene, and I were visiting our family near Charleston, our sporting friends, Mike and Annie, invited us by for a shrimp feast. However, I had to help catch the shrimp.

The routine involved recruiting two new out-of-county boys to hold a big haul seine in chest-deep water as the tide flowed out the river. As one of the novitiates dressed in only a pair of shorts and wading sneakers, I had to laugh as the other new guy holding up the support pole on the shoreward side of the net started yelping in pain as shrimp bumped into his body.

I stopped laughing when the main body of shrimp passed on my side.

Then, I learned how shrimp travel downstream head first. Shrimp have a sharp spike that protrudes from the front of their heads. When punched into human flesh, it hurts.

The other new guy and I put our backs to the current and waited through the suffering till the pricks subsided. Then, we dragged the net ashore to assess our catch. We had caught about eighty pounds of jumbo shrimp!

With a big cooler of shrimp, I skimmed out a couple dozen to take fishing. The local dude fishing on a pier downstream said that was the best place on the river to fish and pulled up a foot long puppy drum to prove it.

Looking down the river, I spotted a steep clay bank with a couple big trees that were lying horizontally in the water.

"Could we use that Boston Whaler to run down the creek to fish over there?" I asked.

"Sure, but the best fishing is right off this dock." the local guy said but obliged my request by producing a set of boat keys.

I anchored the Whaler upstream of the submerged logs and showed the fisherman how to hook a shrimp so that it looked to be running downstream. My first bait drifted below the snags, and I pulled a five-pound Red Drum from the obstructions. The local boy's eyes popped out. "That's the biggest Channel Bass I've ever seen come from this river!" he exclaimed.

"Well, there's a bigger one waiting for you," I replied. Sure enough, a few minutes later, he pulled in a six-pounder. He smiled broadly at the biggest Channel Bass that he had ever caught.

We caught another Channel Bass around three pounds and a big flounder before the tide officially died.

With some fine fish to add to the shrimp feast, we ended the day grilling up our catch and telling fish stories.

Next time you go fishing, stop by your local seafood house and pick up a pound of fresh shrimp to add to your arsenal of tasty fish enticements. Keep those shrimp nice and cold on ice. Should you not catch a fish, you can always eat your bait.

Larry Jarboe - bass21292@yahoo.com

Chapter Twenty Four

Catchin' and Cookin' Muskrat

By Ken Rossignol

When traveling through the scenic small town of Princess Anne, located on Maryland's Eastern Shore, a visitor during the fall might notice the sign advertising the annual Muskrat Dinner.

Surely, at least one trip during the lifespan of a Tidewater resident should be made to the fire department feast of a river rat.

For those lucky enough to have muskrats living along their shoreline and wondering what to do what those critters, a few words about what they are and what they aren't might be helpful.

The fact is that they are really good to eat. With that thought in mind, a couple of ways to cook up these critters is included in this article.

First of all, the name implies that the Muskrat is a rat or that it is musky. Neither is true.

Rats carry disease, muskrats do not. The muskrat is not a marsh rabbit. While it is a very distant cousin of a rat in that it is a rodent, the muskrat lives exclusively in riverbanks and marshes.

A family of muskrat's lives in our seawall and a neighbor is interested in trapping them, but that would remove one of about a dozen determined critters and fowl that call our waterfront yard me from our daily parade of wildlife.

From the upper reaches of the Chesapeake at Harve de Grace down to the tip of Point Lookout, over to the Rappahannock and across to Cape Charles – in every tributary, creek, and river of the Chesapeake region live the muskrat. We could likely feed a small nation if they were all rounded up at once.

The muskrat builds dome-shaped structures of cattails and reeds as well as burrow into river banks to survive the cold and harsh winters of the Chesapeake tidewater region.

The major furriers are well-acquainted with the muskrat. Current prices available online show that muskrat coats may retail between $1,000 and $1,500. Time to get out of the traps!

If planning on shooting your resident muskrat, be careful not to nail him in the back as that is the best fur for making coats.

Muskrat coats are rated to be very warm, much like the mink, which generally costs more. One online fur coat expert gives advice on how to sell grandma's antique muskrat coat and what to expect.

Others might believe shooting a muskrat in the head would be just the ticket. Not so.

When preparing the muskrat meat, first, the hide is removed, leaving the carcass. All of the internal organs are removed as well as the genitalia. Be careful to clean out the cavity up into the neck as well. With no need for the feet, unless one is considering pickling them like pigs' feet, cut them off as well. Cut off the tail, and there could be some uses for that like attaching it to a child's bicycle handlebar.

The head of the muskrat has now been skinned right down to the nose, including removing the eyeballs, extraneous whiskers, and don't forget the ears.

Here is an important step: soak ole Mr. Muskrat in cold saltwater overnight and give it a freshwater bath in the morning.

Now it's time to cut up your muskrat carcass just like you would a chicken. But it won't taste like chicken when you get done with it.

Your muskrat should now be in about seven wonderful pieces to proceed with towards the end result of a great meal.

It is now time to parboil this soon to be connoisseur's delight.

Fire up your kettle and toss the muskrat pieces in with salt and some dried red pepper flakes. Adding in fresh spices from your herb garden is a great addition. Sage, rosemary, thyme, and parsley work well.

One of the reasons for this parboiling is to get the musk out of the rat, and it's a good idea to turn on the fan over your pot during this process. The herbs you added to it will not only help with the flavor but with the odor soon to overtake your kitchen. But you Tidewater folks are a tough lot, and it's a long time until the Princess Anne Fire Department Muskrat Dinner.

Smart chefs follow up the next day with cooking one of the favorite flavorful recipes the next day to replace the muskrat musk with a more pleasing aroma.

Now it's time to get busy cooking your muskrat.

Potted Muskrat

Use any shortening, olive oil, canola, or another fat substitute for good old sausage grease kept in your can under the sink just for such an occasion.

Pull out your old iron skillet and fire it up, add your choice of grease, and on medium heat, cook your muskrat until the meat falls off the bones.

Remove the bones and continue to stir and when it's done, serve it up for dinner.

Pan-fried Muskrat

After draining the par-boiled muskrat, place it in the iron above skillet (if you don't have an iron skillet, how can you call yourself a cook?) with enough of your chosen grease to cover the bottom of the pan. There is no need to use flour or breading, you are cooking with oil! When its browned up and cooked good, its time to ring the dinner bell!

Now since you harvested plenty of meat from the headpiece, especially the thick neck of the muskrat, it's time to consider what to do with the rest of the head – the brain.

People who live down by the marshes assign the task of cracking the skull open to the children. They use a wooden mallet and pluck out the cooked brain meat, which is what the Marsh People call Muskrat Nuggets, and the kids chomp them down with wild abandon. Most adults skip the Muskrat Nuggets except for those like me who love brains & eggs and grits. We obviously will eat anything.

Since you clearly are not in a restaurant, you will have to decide on side dishes yourself.

Fall and winter vegetables include kale, spinach, celery, and cabbage, and with lots of carrots available, as well as sweet potatoes in a variety of ways, your dinner menu is complete. Don't forget to make some cornbread or spoonbread.

This process leaves a tasty meal of good meat, and the

"gameness" was removed by the par-boiling process. This is about the best darn eating you'll ever enjoy.

***

"A noisy man is always in the right."

William Cowper   1731 – 1800

Chapter Twenty Five

***

**The Country
Philosopher
By
Stephen Gore Uhler**

THE AUTHORITY ON
GOOD SENSE

The Country Philosopher

My Lasting Line

By Stephen Gore Uhler

Most great philosophers /authors leave a phrase or sentence that will be connected with them forever.

[Cogito, ergo sum; Je Pense, done Je Suis]

"I think therefore I am," Rene Descartes, of course.

"The play's the thing," who else but William Shakespeare.

Thomas Wolfe penned the simple title, "You can't go home again," which has stayed with us for more than half a century.

I need to coin a phrase for the ages that will always be identified as my work, but I don't have the originality of a Descartes, Shakespeare, or Wolfe.

I will just plagiarize Thomas Wolfe and disguise it with a little paraphrasing.

My words for the ages will be, "You can't stay home, even when you want to."

I ventured out to see the world in my younger days. I saw many opportunities for wealth and fame. Naturally, with my handsome looks and superior talents, I could have chosen the time and place to avail myself of those many opportunities.

But I didn't aspire to wealth and fame in the usual sense of the word.

I wanted to live in St. Mary's County.

My wealth would be a pen of fat hogs and a verdant garden. My fame would be only known to my fellow Countians.

I cared not what lay north of Hughesville. In those halcyon days of the '40s and 50, are the outside yahoos didn't care about St. Mary's County, and we didn't care about them. We had the "Land of Pleasant Living" all to ourselves with room to stretch out and roam uncluttered fields and beaches, to drive open roads.

Happy and free.

I would never leave home.

But then in the 1960s, the blacks got uppity and started moving to the white suburbs. The yahoo whites decided to flee to terra incognita, that wild, unsettled land inhabited by a few illiterate inbreds.

And down the stretch, they came. Ashen faced lemmings, pouring down Rt. 235.

We didn't have room in this little peninsula for all those refugees and all their "necessities."

The first thing they needed was dualized highways. Our little 16-foot Macadams were not sufficient for their driving habits.

Then they needed stoplights.

What was wrong with our old traffic rule of "stop, look, and listen?" We already had one stoplight on Duke's Corner that nobody obeyed anyway.

Then the dumb sumbitches couldn't find their way around. They needed house numbers. Planning and zoning bowed to their wishes and put a street number on every shack and shanty in the county.

My farm has six different house numbers.

I refuse to put up any of them.

The banks, post offices, and business places are amused when I can't tell them where I live after being here for 3/4 of a century.

I carry a list of street numbers in my wallet, but I can't remember which number fits my house and which is my barn or hog pen.

No, Mr. Wolfe, I didn't try to come home again, I never left. My home left me.

The biggest loss when my County left me was the open roads.

On my 16th birthday, I applied for a driver's license and was issued a learner's card, which I didn't really need. I had been driving for years. Two weeks later, I was issued my Maryland operator's license, which has remained unblemished in my wallet for 50 years.

As soon as I had my license in my pocket, my mother asked me if I would try to teach my older sister.

"Your dear sister wants to drive in the worst way."

I figured she already drove in the worst way, but Mama had asked me, so I took on the task.

A lot of good instructors had tried and failed with my sister. She could go through all the motions while in our yard, but when she met an oncoming car on the road, she had the nasty habit of letting go of the wheel and clasping her hands over her eyes, which behavior caused a lot of good instructors to quit.

I figured we had a good training route. There were a mile and a half from our house to Hill's Store, open fields all the way. Our farm had a frontage on Rt. 238 of 3/4 mile. The Woodley Morgan Farm was more than a 1-mile frontage. The rest of the route was covered by Dr. Johnson's huge fields on the south side of 238.

I would tell my sister not to close her eyes even if she met one of those big Bailey's Express rigs, all she does, if she panicked, was cut right and put her in the field.

As an inducement to get me to train my sister, my father had purchased a brand new 1950 Chevy Fleetline. Daddy wouldn't have a radio in it. He figured if you were out to drive, then drive. If you wanted to listen to the radio, then you should sit home with him and Mama and listen to the radio.

It had turn signals on the column; you didn't have to wind the window down to signal your turns. It needed some mud flaps with chrome stars and some of those stick-on portholes, but I would buy them myself as soon as the tobacco market opened. Dr. Johnson's big Roadmaster Buick had those chrome portholes in the fender, and it was the classiest car in the neighborhood.

My sister and I set out for our first drive.

I rehearsed over and over with her how she could turn the wheel right and, "Put 'er in the field."

Sister was driving right along until she got to Woodley Morgan's gate, and an oncoming car popped up over the rise. True to her training, my panicked sister, "put 'er in the field."

Then I remembered there was only one obstruction on that stretch of road for a mile and a half. There was a little spring that rose up by Woodley Morgan's gate, a little net bog of swamp grass and elderberries.

True to Murphy's Law, my sister put that shiny new Chevy right in the middle of the spring. I walked home to get our old John Deere. The Magneto was wet, the sumbitch wouldn't start. I would have to put the harness on old "Doll."

"Doll" was a big powerful mare; she was wind broke and couldn't work long without a rest. By the time that I had harnessed old Doll and walked her back to the car, it had settled tight down on the frame.

I hooked old Doll to the back bumper, the only place I could get to.

"Git up, Doll." She danced in the harness a few times to test the weight and gave it her mightiest lunge.

The bumper came off, and Doll took off.

All the way home with that shiny chrome bumper bouncing on her heels.

I don't need to say Papa was not pleased. His new car torn up, his best mare cut up. Papa was not pleased, and for as long as she lived, Doll would not allow herself to be hitched to a vehicle.

Yes, we had those little malfunctions on our open roads back in the "good old days," but nothing to equal those glutted highways, with stoplights every 50 feet and those satanic numbers affixed to every dwelling.

I was driving home the other day, stopping every 50 feet for one of those damned lights, trying to fight off the incipient Road Rage. I tried to calm myself by telling myself that the county is as low as it can get.

Those outside sumbitches have ruined our Fair County. There is nothing else they can do.

Forget it. I'll soon be at home.

As I turned into Hollywood, I saw the forms: *Curb forms*.

They're going to put city curbs right here in River City.

We can't even "put 'er in the field" anymore.

We are trapped here in this ribbon of asphalt with lights in front and behind and curbs on both sides.

You're right, Mr. Wolfe, you can't go home again, nor can you stay home.

"It is elementary, my dear Watson," -- A. C. Doyle
***

"When I want to read a novel, I write one."

Benjamin Disraeli   1804-1881

Chapter Twenty-Six

Spiced Shrimp, Fresh Fish, and Oysters

Keep Pee Wee and Ralph Gray Hopping

By Ken Rossignol

NEW MARKET --- Frances "Pee Wee" Gray, co-owner of Copsey Leonard Market on Rt. 5 in New Market operates a busy seafood carryout that caters to a clientele of long-time native residents as well as those motoring in Southern Maryland that are lucky enough to spot the sign for the business.

"I've been working around it since I was little, it seems like it's been forever. I started out helping my father, buying crabs as a teen. In 1974, I went to work for him full time, he used to have the Famous Drift Inn Crab House, the oldest in southern Maryland. He had the Crab House in the summer and oysters in the winter and grew tobacco in the summers too," said Gray.

Two of her sisters and her brother all operate thriving seafood restaurants in the St. Mary's County. Sissy operates the Sandgates Inn on the Patuxent River, her brother Lonnie and his wife Elaine operate Captain Leonard's Crabhouse on Rt. 235 in Oraville, and her sister Pumpkin and her husband Jerry Bowles own and operate her parent's long-time business, Drift Inn.

"Yes. I grew up near the Patuxent River on a farm; it was six girls and one boy, and we were all the help that my father had, that's why he had us," Pee-Wee said with a laugh. "In the summer months, we had crab pickers who would work six days a week picking crab meat, and on the seventh day, we would drive all over the county to pick the crabs up and bring them back to the Crab House. We sold a lot of our crabs to the Belvedere Restaurant in Lexington Park, which is gone now, and other local restaurants."

"In the winter, we had the oyster business. We would buy oysters every day, 150 to 200 bushels, we had oodles of oysters. With all the oysters I saw, I never thought I would live to see no oysters, but they began dying out in the '80s. A lot of stores that we sold oysters to went out of business, and it was a gradual downhill slide, but now it's basically gone. The oysters got a disease which is killing them, and there are very few left."

Pee Wee has a point of view on what happened to the oysters.

"When bad water comes in, fish and crabs can move away, but an oyster stays where it is. Oysters filter water and try to clean it out, but now it's killing them to do it. Pollution is a big problem, but I don't know what can be done about it. The oil spill we had in the Patuxent about thirteen years ago didn't help either. Now they are trying to bring in oysters from Asia that are supposed to be resistant to the disease our oysters have."

As to whether or not oysters will ever return to the days of being so plentiful, such as in the late 1800s that they were considered 'white gold,' she notes there will be a real problem in how to process them as the workforce has changed dramatically.

"Well, if they do come back, I don't know who is going to do it. Most of the shuckers are gone, most of them are old and can't do it anymore, and the young people, they won't do it. Now we get most of our oysters from other places, like Texas, Louisiana, and Mississippi. And now the crabs are going the way of the oysters, they're not as big and not as plentiful."

"They have farm-raised catfish now if they could farm raise crabs, I would buy stock in that, it would be like Microsoft. But there would be so much to it, I don't know if we'll ever see a crab farm, but if we did, we'd have it made. The problem now is that we don't know what we're going to get; big crabs, small, alive, dead, fat, lightweight. I got into this part of the business because the oyster industry was dying. There were less and less supply and less demand, and I just couldn't survive in the oyster packing house anymore, now we sell fish, fillets, crabs, and all kinds of stuff, not just one product."

True to her word, Ralph and Pee Wee's store now carries about every type of seafood spice that exists, including utensils such as crab mallets, oyster knives, and condiments. If it's made for preparing fish and seafood, Leonard Copsey's Seafood Market has it in stock, along with cold beer and liquor.

"This is a dying business, my kids won't have to worry about doing this," said Pee Wee. "You can't really get into this kind of business because it just won't be here for long. My main thing here is crabs, and now they are going. It's getting harder and harder because there are fewer crabs, they cost me more, and I make less profit. I have to throw out a lot of dead crabs these days; I lose money on every one of those. Every spring, I have to ask myself: will I get enough crabs to get through the next season? We had this hurricane a few years back, Hurricane Isabel in 2003, which stirred the water up real good; I had hoped it might help us out."

Customers have their preferences for seafood, and one asked Pee Wee on Christmas Eve where the oysters came from. She told him from the Patuxent River and satisfied, he left with a couple of quarts. The salinity of the oysters can vary along with the size. Private oyster beds are treasured leases in various locations, and State of Maryland oyster seeding programs have provided some success stories as well as criminal cases of poaching.

But life on the Chesapeake and its tributaries is a lot different from the days of oyster wars when Maryland and Virginia watermen routinely engaged in gun battles at sea with fatalities. In some cases, oyster pirates fired on police boats. A Virginia governor actually formed a fleet to surround Maryland oyster pirates and bring them to justice, with varying degrees of success.

With her parents now in their nineties and Ralph retired from the phone company, their small business keeps them working long hours six days a week. They take a month off in the dead of winter and crank right back up again.

"I was born into this business, and it's all I know. Like these watermen here, it's all they know. All their lives, they've been doing this, working hard at it and struggling. We don't want to lose it, it's a Southern Maryland thing, oysters, and crabs, that's what Southern Maryland stands for."

Pee Wee says that the younger generation doesn't eat seafood like those that came before them.

"The oyster business used to be rocking and rolling, we would sell them as fast as we could shuck them, to DC, to Virginia," said Pee Wee. "We had seven or eight shuckers working five days a week and shucking 150 bushels a day. Now, these young people, they just don't eat oysters like the old people did. You don't walk into McDonald's and see oyster nuggets because people don't eat it. And a lot of younger people don't eat the crabs anymore either."

"When I first opened, it took some time to build this up. We had a seafood place like this across the street, and one down the road, and it's hard to build up when you're right on top of the competition. It was hard, but it's a lot better now, and there are so many people in this county now."

"When you were born and raised here, there was nothing here, but St. Mary's has boomed, it's exploded. The growth is incredible, who would have thought we'd have so many Wawa's in one little county?"

"Now everything is a super chain store, like Kohl's, Wal-Mart, Target or K-Mart. A lot of the mom and pop stores have gone out since the big chains came in," she said. "There's a big difference, though, and the personal touch is gone."

"St. Mary's has always been supported by a mom and pop places, nice family owned and local. Local owners can interact with customers on a personal level; you don't see that in a chain store. You go to a chain restaurant, and you feel like a number; you go in, sit down, eat, and get out. People don't want to stay, but if they go to a place where they feel welcome, people will stay all night."

Underlining the change in St. Mary's County, the old traditional eating establishments in Lexington Park and Leonardtown are history. Gone are the Belvedere, The Roost, Pete's Galley, the Willows, and the Half Way House.

Fighting the trend is just a handful of holdouts, such as Billy Hill's St. Mary's Landing, Fitzie's Marina, and the restaurants operated by the Copsey siblings.

In California and Lexington Park, the parking lots stay full at the various Mexican restaurants and the row of chain eateries along Rt. 235.

"Business isn't what it used to be," said Pee Wee. "It's a lot harder to find help, good help, that is. There's plenty of help out there, but you don't know what you're going to get. My son Ralph Jr. used to help out, but he works for an elevator company now, it's a stable living. It's sad, I would be more than happy to pass this business along, but it's just not feasible, this is going the same way as farms, and most people can't survive by farming anymore.

With just one employee, who has been with them for more than fifteen years, Pee Wee and Ralph find that they do have an intensely personal connection with their customers. Peak business hours keep all three of them working in overdrive to keep the orders flowing out the door while watermen make deliveries at the back door.

They stay busy frying, steaming and cooking sandwiches and orders of seafood to go along with oysters shucked or in the shell. Long cases display fresh fish fillets, scallops, shellfish, and shrimp, making the seafood market one of the few places for customers to pick out their dinner and wait for it to be cooked to perfection or simply packaged for them and put in ice for a trip home to be cooked.

(In 2019, Pee Wee and Ralph retired and closed their business.)

Unloading oysters at Rock Point, Md. *Library of Congress*

Chapter Twenty-Seven

The Country Philosopher

The Commies Stole My Hole Card

By Stephen Gore Uhler

Any of you folks who are of my generation might remember Joe BTZFLK. Joe was a creation of Al Capp, who wrote and drew the Lil' Abner comic strip.

Al Capp created numerous characters in his strip. There was the "Schmoo," a loveable character which infected the whole U.S. There was a schmoo café or schmoo diner in just about every town.

In Joe BTZFLK, Capp created the born loser, the most unlucky, depressed little character you ever saw. In fact, he was always portrayed with his own personal storm cloud, which followed him wherever he went. The scene in the comic strip could be bright and sunny, but when Joe BTZFLK appeared, he would bring his personal cloud with him, soaking him, and only him with a dreary, cold drizzle.

I am sure Al Capp patterned his characters after real-life persons. I know in my writing, whenever I create some outlandish character, it is always based somewhat on a real person I have met somewhere along the way.

Al Capp was known to travel a lot. I don't know whether he ever came to St. Mary's County, but somehow he must have met me at some time. I am Joe BTZFLK, born to lose.

As the old black folk used to say, "If it were rainin' soup, you'd show up with a fork."

The old adage says, "Lucky at cards, unlucky at love" or vice versa.

Not true. I have been left penniless at the card table with a busted flush and watched my favorite babe slinking out the door with a new man she had found while I was fighting those bad cards to provide her with the better things in life.

Life ain't fair, adages ain't true.

Despite the slings and arrows that have assailed since the moment of my birth, I have never allowed myself to become a quitter. I will work harder, try harder, I will survive. I will never be a victim.

Every venture I entered into wound up a failure, not a failure of my making, just some calamitous failure, sort of a titanic-iceberg syndrome.

I have watched hail flatten my tobacco the day before harvest, and sleet shredded my peach orchard the spring before my first harvest. The year I tried hogs, the market crashed. I sunk thousands in the purchase of an Edsel dealership.

Just a born loser, no other term for it.

My siblings, who went forth into the world and immediately began to pile up huge savings accounts and retirement plans, cast worried glances at my futile attempts to attain financial security.

"Stephen, you have to plan more carefully. You are going to wind up in your old age flat broke. Quit your whoring, drinking, and gambling and invest in something secure."

I had to laugh at their worries. They hadn't peeped at my hole cards. I held two aces down.

My first ace was my natural-born talent as a writer, and my second ace was the farm that I had bought at an early age and watched double in value year by year.

I could always sit down and write out a short story and sell it, or if I got tired of writing, I could always sell off an acre or two. I had absolutely no reason to worry.

I never heard of Hemmingway missing any meals. Faulkner died in a mansion, Shakespeare had no problem selling his product.

Hell, I could make big money writing T.V. scripts. I know all the lewd, scatological four-letter words, I am familiar with every sexual position; I could write T.V. scripts with one hand tied behind my back.

But a fellow might get tired of writing, as easy as it is. My big hole card, the black ace was my real estate.

Let me take you to the most prominent hill on my ranch, look out in four directions. What appears as far as your eyes can see? You see the land. Land bought and paid for by Stephen G. Uhler in the wisdom of his youth, all tillable and perkable.

The present value, …you ask?

It's value on today's market, with all the yahoos crowding into our fair county? Let me think a while.

Kaching! Kaching!

Let's just say I don't need to worry.

Unlike Joe BTSFLK, who could never elude his cloud, I had out-paced mine. There was bright sunshine for the rest of my days.

I didn't realize that our Board of County Commissioners had found my errant cloud and sent it hurrying to find me.

You know how we as kids used to see figures in the clouds, "There's a rabbit," and look, there's a man smoking a pipe."

Well, when my gloom cloud caught up with me, it was in the shape of a 20-acre parcel of land.

The county commissioners had with the stroke of a pen changed me from a prosperous country squire, well prepared for his old age to a penniless old dependent, a broken-down, food stamp licking old bum.

I know that when we went outside for our commissioners that we were asking for trouble, but I didn't think it would affect me so directly.

I thought it hilarious that in 1998, our commissioners would be led by a henna-headed "Bama gal" with cotton lint under her fingernails and peanut grease on her chin.

Ably assisted by a washed-out Vista volunteer ex-patriot from Connecticut who studied his politics under V. I. Lenin.

I didn't worry too much about the cute little woman from "Joisy." She passed herself off as a "Reagan Republican; she had been smart enough to catch a practitioner of the Medical Arts for a husband. She wouldn't do much harm.

I should have paid more attention. This zoning crap should have been killed in the womb, but too many landowners were too busy to see what was coming.

So now I am stuck with this albatross; this worthless piece of land that I am too arthritic to farm, too blind to look across and enjoy and prevented from selling by a yahoo bunch of commissioners.

I thought at this point in my life that I would ride off into the sunset, with coins jingling on my spurs, singing "Happy Trails to you." Instead, I'll be plodding along, penniless, with this ever-present black cloud drizzling on my head singing "Born to Lose."

Hit it on the Dobro, Joe.

Chapter Twenty Eight

The Adventures of Studs

Bowhunting the Bear

By E. V. Roderick

One of these days I'm going to do it again. I'm going to find my old split limb compound bow, gather up a few hunting arrows and head back to the mountains of New England. I'm going to knock on the door of the hunting guide and tell him to take me up the mountain to where the Olde Blackie lives. After ten years, I can hardly live with myself. Shamed by a mere bear, I can hardly tell the story.

It was about ten years ago that I accepted an invitation to hunt the elusive black bear. Being an avid female archer, the menfolk had attended my every need in teaching me the necessary skills to become a hunter.

At first, it was difficult because hunting is predominantly a male sport. The equipment used is designed by men and catered to their physical abilities. Not many years ago, a longbow with enough energy to bring down big game, like a whitetail deer, would have to pull at 75 pounds at full draw. This was nearly the same equipment used by soldiers of the Middle Ages and back into Biblical times. Next came the fiberglass recurve bow, still a bit to draw, but lighter and faster than the longbow, it really opened the door for women.

… at the maximum level, a well-placed arrow can bring down any big game…

A used Bear Kodiak fiberglass recurve in 45 lb. draw was my first hunting bow. Having just stepped up from a 30 lb. Target Model, it was hard at first and became easier as I practiced and practiced.

Sunday afternoons after church, Studs, my husband, and I would go to informal shoots at our hunting buddy's home. Finally, with a lot of practice, I could pluck most targets, still or moving with the best of them. My hunting buddies, of course, had long ago conceded, in spite of their male egos, that I was becoming a crack shot. The first year I hunted with a bow, I got a small buck. I field dressed it, and packed it out of the woods myself, without nary a male assistant. After that, the men in the hunting camp just treated me like one of the boys.

Along the second year of bowhunting, my darling husband gave me a compound bow for Christmas. To most women, this act wouldn't have gone one over too well, but for me, it was really swelling. A compound bow is one that by its design, its easy to hold at full draw and yet shoots faster. It shoots farther, flatter, and most importantly, it is adjustable up to 65 lbs. of force. At the maximum level, a well-placed arrow can bring down any big game in North America. Charging elephants have been killed with less. I was ecstatic! The adventure with the compound began shortly after New Year's Day. A hunting club decided to book a week in the mountains of New England in the spring for Black Bear. This left me but a little time to get used to the new bow and tone up my back muscles. By the Spring, I was using sixty pounds regularly. Boy, did that new bow, impress me.

At eighty yards with sights, I could keep the shots in a 14" diameter paper plate. At fifty in a paper soup bowl, and at thirty in a teacup. Inside 20 yards, the arrow was sure to go through the eye of the cup handle. To the men, this level of skill was nearly magical. No woman was ever supposed to shoot like that: wanting to admit that my eye-hand coordination was at least as good as theirs, would eventually descent to muttering that, "She can shoot, but can she handle the pressure of a charging bear?"

Rabbits, yes, bears – well, maybe! Long ago, I got over trying to prove myself to men, but that one remark about the bear hung in my mind.

In preparation for the Gold Bear Expedition, Studs and I read every magazine article about black bears we could find. Two things troubled me the most. A female bear will almost attack anything that gets too close to her cubs. And, even with a heart, shot out by an arrow, a black bear can take up to eight seconds to collapse. In this time, the fatally wounded animal can charge a hunter and run a hundred yards or more.

Since most bow shots are about thirty yards distance, it was readily apparent to me that if the bear charged the archer (on the ground), somebody was likely to get hurt. For this reason, climbing trees became part of my routine before the hunt. Studs thought I'd lost it.

On the appointed weekend, Studs, the hunting club, and I drove up to New England and met the guide at about 9 p.m. that night. He told us to sack until 4 a.m. when we could be taken to our stands. Still sleepy in the darkness, we later loaded onto a flatbed trailer behind a tractor, and the guide took us up to the mountain. Not exactly our classic hayride. En route, he told us to look for Old Blackie. The guide lowered his voice as he described in Satanic terms about a large Black Bear that had been marauding livestock in the valley, and that one of his clients had wounded the demon a couple of days earlier.

"If you see Blackie," whispered the guide," Wait till he turns away from you before you shoot. That way, if you hit him, he's not able to charge you if he doesn't know where it came from."

The other hunters were silent at this remark, and the tractor chug-chugged up the trail in the cold darkness. Now and then, they'd stop, and the guide would usher an expectant hunter into the bush, out of sight or hearing, and return alone a few minutes later.

When it became my turn, the guide whisked me along, through huckleberries as high as my knees, to a ledge about eight feet up a rock outcropping. There was a putrid smell in the air, and the path along the cliff was narrow and slippery. Without the use of a light, I stumbled along not knowing how high up we were, certain one false step would send me falling to a bottomless descent. Once situated on the ledge, the guide told me when dawn came, I would find myself overlooking a clearing and bait heap of rolling fish. If a bear appeared, said he, it would come straight out of the hucks from the far side.

Then, the guide left.

It was cold. As the gray of dawn began to break the night, it illuminated by position, or should I say situation. The ledge I was on was a four by a six-foot stone shelf with barely enough room to stand.

Precariously, it perched on out with a clear view of 180 degrees out to about thirty yards. Stand with the back to the wall, the cliff rose at least fifty feet above me straight up. Here I was stranded, without any place to go, not even up. All that tree climbing wasn't going to help me. I stood motionless, looking out over the stinking fish. And then something caught my eye. Down. Just below my feet on the ground was a fuzzy black boulder – only it moved. I could see it better now. Its shape was coming straight below me a scant ten yard out. Now, six. I froze I couldn't move. I didn't dare even wink. My heart was pounding in my ears. I prayed the bear wouldn't look up and see the little puffs of breath vapors I was trying to blow down my shirt. With my bow braced one end on the ledge and the other in my hand, I knew if the animal lunged at me, I'd never get a shot off.

Eventually, the black mass lumbered down along the base of the rocks, passing a mere four feet below me before heading for the bait pile. Why he didn't smell me, I'll never know.

I think somewhere else along in here I made a silent deal with that bear. If he didn't hurt me, it wasn't going to bother him. He dragged a couple of fish down through the bush, and I caught up on my breathing. About ten minutes later, I could move a little but was stiff from being all tensed up. At the appointed time, here came the guide with a sack of bait to freshen up the pile. My, what some people will do for a dollar. Anyway, the guide, of course, wanted to know about, "Did I see the bear?"

"Yes, I said," then thinking quickly, "Well, actually, No. I feel asleep –uh- from the long drive and all."

"Too bad," said the guide, "That's Olde Blackie's mark, by the heap, would have been a fine shot."

Of course, when we all get back into camp, it turned out I was the only hunter who had a chance at all. Everyone else had struck out. I faked the flu for the next three days and stayed in camp.

But this year I'm going back, with Studs of course. We've signed up for the rock-climbing classes beforehand. I'll tell Stud's way later.

***

"Freedom has a thousand charms to show; That slaves, however, contented, never know."
William Cowper 1731 – 1800
***

Chapter Twenty Nine

Tony Averella enjoys a state park built on the old Rt. 50 highway bridge over the Choptank River.

THE CHESAPEAKE TODAY photo

Tidewater Park on a Bridge

Choptank River Bridge Retained as Fishing Pier After New Bridge Eliminated Draw Span

By Ken Rossignol

CAMBRIDGE, MD. --- In spite of all the great destinations along the Delmarva shore, some folks decide that poking around Pocomoke City, taking an island cruise from either Point Lookout or Crisfield to Tangier and Smith Islands or fishing from a pier jutting out over the Choptank is for them.

One such fellow is Tony Averella, of Baltimore. Tony had been working his assortment of crab traps from his post along the two-mile-long fishing pier at the Choptank River on July 21st until deciding to pack up about noon following a close encounter with a turtle.

This particular turtle came very close to being in Tony's soup pot at the worst, or only being measured and photographed at the very least, but in any event, this turtle was well fed as he is a prime suspect in the larceny of all the bait from several crab traps.

Tony relates that he was pulling up one trap loaded with the turtle when he got it nearly to the pier, and the line snapped. Down went trap and turtle and all.

The day was slow for crabbing with two prime keepers on ice, and many small crabs and females tossed back.

The pier is the old U. S. 50 drawbridge over the Choptank at Cambridge and was retained as a mecca for fisherfolks due to the hard work and leadership of the famed late Baltimore Sun fishing writer Bill Burton.

The State was prepared to remove the entire bridge structure and demolish it when Burton led the effort to keep the bridge and just remove the draw span.

The remainder, in two sections, now serves the public as a state park entirely over water, one of the few in the region, and allows fisherfolks to gain access to prime fishing without having to own a boat.

Adults must have Maryland fishing licenses for fish and for crabbing. It helps to have kids to haul stuff for the family on the long trek out on the bridge, and due to the paved surface, the bridge is an ideal place for the disabled to scoot out for a day of fishing, providing one can use a porta-potty.

There are several picnic tables with covers, and those fishing can always bring their own umbrellas along with coolers on wheels. No booze is allowed at the Bill Burton State Park.

The only traffic on the pier is that created by people, while the new bridge nearby carries autos and trucks, and commercial fishing boats provide plenty to look at while waiting for the fish to bite.

Tony has been fishing the pier for a long time and was there many times over the years when it was still carrying traffic across the river.

"We often caught various those old blowfish and horseshoe crabs which were hard to get off your lines, but a slight backhand of the rod brought the end of the line into the line of traffic, and by the end of the day there was a lot of fish along the curb," said Tony.

Nowadays, those fishing from the pier will have to deal with unwanted catches differently.

The pier reaching out over the river from the Cambridge side is much shorter than from the Talbot County side of the pier.

Tony recalls that everyone on the eastern shore side of the

Chesapeake Bay knew Bill Burton and had met him at one fishing spot or another.

He said that Burton got his best tips in bars when liquored up fishermen revealed their best fishing holes and strategies.

"You would open the paper, and there it was right in his column," said Averella.

The 1992 legislation authorizing for the first time, the creation of a saltwater fishing license for recreational fishing, was designated to have the funds used for establishing fish reefs and fishing piers in Maryland.

The people of the State of Maryland got a great bargain in keeping the Choptank River Bridge and reusing the resource for moving traffic into recreation, mainly due to the efforts of Bill Burton.

Maryland seldom names anything for anyone other than a politician. In this case, the name fits the legacy.

A family fishing day at the Bill Burton Fishing Pier over the Choptank River at Cambridge, Md. *THE CHESAPEAKE TODAY photo*

Chapter Thirty

Fishing for Freedom

By Cap'n Larry Jarboe

Until the yellow perch start its run in March, there is a very limited fishing opportunity in Maryland. I might slip into the Chalk Point Power Plant to catch some fat channel cats over the next few weeks, but mostly, there is a lifetime of stories to relate and a new GPS that I have to figure how to work. And, dozens of different, good eating species of fish are waiting to bite on my line further south where the water is warmer.

There is plenty of time for me to plan my next boat and methods of fishing and/or crabbing. Already, Mike Murray has the hull poured for my next boat, a 15-foot 9-inch long crabbing skiff powered by a 24-volt inboard permanent magnet DC motor with a full skeg keel and a steering cup around the prop for super maneuverability. The T-top will have two fixed solar panels overhead to provide shade for me and free energy for the bank of golf cart batteries.

Why build a boat less than 16 feet long?

The Maryland boat registration fee for boats less than 16 feet powered by less than 7 ½ horsepower is free. That's a pretty good reason.

Fishing can be as cheap as putting a worm on a hook and line with a bobber above and extending it out into a farm pond on a cane pole. Crabbing from a pier with baited lines and a dip net is also a pretty darned inexpensive way to spend a day. Once we bring a boat into the picture, it gets exponentially more expensive. Then, the government wants its share.

When my two friends applied for their three-day saltwater fishing license at the K-Mart in Florida, the young clerk from Michigan said that he could not afford to fish. The non-resident saltwater annual license is $47.50.

I remember when you could fish anywhere in saltwater for free. You could sell your bucket of fish to whatever fish house or restaurant that wanted to buy them without having to buy out someone else's commercial license or licenses. Why are we driving another generation away from the sport or business of fishing with both exorbitant expenses and obtrusive regulations?

Sensible rules to protect fish stocks benefit us all. The ban on catching female crabs and wintertime crab dredging were long overdue. However, allowing one fisherman to take only two striped basses while someone who has been grandfathered or negotiated the maze of paperwork can capture hundreds of pounds reeks of unfairness. There must be a simpler way to conserve our fish stocks while promoting recreational and commercial fishing for future generations. Florida did it with a net ban twenty years ago, but they have an even greater quagmire of expenses and confusing regulations for law-abiding citizens to attempt to adhere to due to the additional encroachment of Federal jurisdiction into waters three miles offshore.

One Florida Federal Marine Police Officer confided to me in a pre-dawn coffee conversation at the Circle-K, "We board a boat figuring that everyone is doing something illegal."

Following in the footsteps of Michener and Hemmingway, as the most prolific living writer of fishing stories from the Chesapeake Bay to the Keys, I would like to see young people have the opportunity to experience the same freedom and adventure that I have been able to enjoy. Let us all work together and plan this winter that each year will be the year we fish for freedom for the next generation. We have the opportunity to free ourselves from the elected leadership of a Federal Government that has turned us into a Country of rules so extensive that "everyone is doing something illegal."

Take this time to rig up a couple of cane poles to take your children or grandchildren fishing in a farm pond (with permission from the owner, of course). Plan to take those kids in their lifejackets on a pier to go crabbing. If you have a boat in Maryland, pay the fifty bucks for the fishing license that covers the whole boat and dedicate yourself to introducing as many novices as you can to the delightfully natural pastimes of fishing and/or crabbing in the Chesapeake watershed. The same license in Florida costs $2,001.50. Yes, you read it right, $2,001.50! There are still good deals to be had in Maryland, but don't tell our State legislators.

Please share your fishing, boating, hunting, and other outdoor stories with our friends and neighbors by forwarding your written exploits to bass21292@yahoo. We look forward to having you fish for freedom with us.

You are also free to stretch the truth a bit.

Cap'n Larry Jarboe - bass21292@yahoo.com

A day fishing under the new Choptank River Bridge at Cambridge, Md.

THE CHESAPEAKE TODAY photo

Chapter Thirty-One

Cabin Fever:
Real Men Don't Show It
When They Are Hurt

By Stephen Gore Uhler

I always assumed that Cabin Fever only afflicted trappers, prospectors, and such types for months at a time, somewhere high up in the Arctic mountains.

Wintertime never used to bother me. It was a busy time, tobacco to strip, cattle to feed, wood to split, and bring in. I always enjoyed the crispness of the winter air, free of stinging bugs and other crawly things; I even learned to enjoy the sting of sleet on my face, rather invigorating.

The experts who study such things seem to think that the depression of cabin fever is caused by the shortness of daylight rather than the cold temperature, which makes sense. The millionaires skiing on the slopes of Vail and Aspen in below zero temperature don't exhibit any symptoms of depression.

Anyway, that will be my excuse for not writing in the last issue. Cabin Fever, sure enough. But I shouldn't complain; I brought in on myself.

I was brought up back in the good old days when crying was for girls and old ladies. Boys didn't admit to injury. They jumped up from the injury and "played hurt," as the athletes say.

Grown-ups impressed manhood upon their boys at an early age.

"Quit sniveling, you little bastard, you ain't hurt."

And by example:

Back in the good old days before weed eaters and leaf blowers, those chores had to be done with scythes and rakes to cut the weeds and brush back. The scythes had to be razor-sharp.

One day my father was honing his scythe, making long, bold strokes with the file along the long curved blade. Now, it was my job as his able 8-year old assistant to hold the S-shaped scythe just in the right position so that my father could make those bold, sweeping strokes with the file.

I was holding firmly to the scythe, knowing that if I let it slip, he would whip my butt.

Well, as luck would have it, my mind wandered, the scythe wiggled. The sweaty file slipped in Pop's hand, and the keen edge of the scythe took the last joint of my father's finger as clean as a whistle.

He retrieved his bloody file and resumed filing more vigorously than before.

"Daddy, you did cut your finger off."

"Shut up, boy, if you talk about it, it will start hurting."

So that was the macho attitude I assumed. You could follow me around the farm by the gobs of blood and chips of bone and teeth I left behind.

"Are you hurt, man?"

"Just a scratch."

So, it was only a natural reaction a few weeks ago when I fell off my bulldozer and hung there tangled in the shift levers until the nice lady came and cut me loose.

My response was, "I ain't hurt."

"Are you sure?"

"Naw, I ain't hurt."

But as I limped away, I began to feel little bolts of pain running up and down my back. The next morning my hip socket was frozen.

I knew my hip was busted, but I didn't want to tell anybody. President Reagan had broken his hip on the same day, and his injury was in all the headlines, and I knew if I told anybody about my injury, that people would say I was just trying to act Presidential.

So, I dragged my crippled body around the farm from the barn to barn, the stock must be fed. I put out the word to all of my "friends" that I needed help with the feeding.

I waited and waited. I found out how many friends I had.

There I was, my animals starving, and I was freezing. My woodpile is only 50 feet from my house, but I couldn't manage an armful of wood and the crutches too.

I knew I couldn't manage to feed several lots of animals, so I turned my ewes and new lambs in with the horses and somehow dragged bales of hay where they could get it.

The horses were pretty careful around the lambs, but I knew that in the competition for hay that there was a good chance that a lamb would be stepped on.

Oh, the unbearable depression...cold ashes in the hearth, hungry animals bleating and whinnying from the barn.

All I could do was lay there day after day watching the Senate confirmation hearing. When Senator Kennedy would puff himself up and start his bloviating, I didn't even have the strength to throw my boot through the tube.

I could see the cabinet across the room, full of shotguns and shells. Maybe I should just take myself out of the competition.

But no, I am a survivor. My Mama didn't raise no cowards. I'll; hang on 'til spring.

Finally, I got to where I could hobble around the pasture on my crutches, and sure enough, there were two of my fattest lambs, horse stomped.

There was nothing I could do about it. I had done my best.

I was back on my feet. I was able to get a fire going and had been presented with the ingredients for the stomped mutton stew.

Recipe for stomped mutton stew:

l. Skin out the lamb and cut away any bruised carcass. Cut into pieces and bring to a boil.

2. Add salt and black pepper (use more pepper if the lamb has been dead for a while)

3. Add vegetables in the order of cooking time:

Carrots

Celery

Pearled barley

Onions

Potatoes

Allow your fire to die down and maintain just enough coals to maintain a slow simmer.

Chapter Thirty-Two

Fred McCoy stands at the edge of his farm on the shores of the Potomac River.

Letter from St. Gabriel's Manor
Squirrels and Doves

By Frederick L. McCoy

When I was about twelve years old, my father received a substantial raise in salary. That Christmas, he gave each of his children twenty dollars to purchase his own present, a generous gift in 1927. I wanted a shotgun, and during the holidays, one of my older sisters took me and several of the children to the outskirts of Baltimore in her Model T Ford.

Here was the big new mail-order Montgomery Ward's Store. It's first two stories were for local shoppers, the others for mail orders.

The store had a large gun section, and my older brother helped me select a double-barreled 16-gauge Hercules shotgun. It cost all but not more than my twenty-dollar bill. I also purchased two boxes of Red-Head shells, one high-powered and one low, one with #6 size shot for rabbits and squirrels and 7 1/2 for partridges (quail).

The gun was beautiful but heavy for me, and when my father saw it, he scolded my brother for encouraging me to get such a heavy gun. He finally said, "Well, I guess he will grow, and a gun like this is for a lifetime."

The season for squirrel and dove opened on September 1st. I had been anxiously awaiting the opening day for months, but now there was a problem. Papa had taken off from work and had planned a day's outing. He was taking the younger part of the family down to Point Lookout, St. Mary's County, in his big REO Sedan. I told him I could not go as hunting season was opening. He understood and did not insist.

Early September 1st, I was up at first light and off to a little hogback ridge on our farm. There were several hickory nut trees there, and I noticed that the squirrels had started cutting on the nuts. Portions of the nuts were under the trees.

I hid myself as best as I could and remained still. It seemed forever before I heard a squirrel in the distance. Then they came swinging through the trees from branch to branch. I clutched my gun tightly and did not move. Soon one was in the tree above me. I took aim and fired. He fell to the ground. I picked up my quarry and started home to show him to those who were there. As I climbed over another ridge, I walked very slowly because there was an old chestnut tree there. Some of its limbs had died from the blight, and doves often landed on those dead branches. My luck was in. There on top of the branch was a dove, and I shot – down he came, but of all things, there had been another dove just behind him, and I picked up two, not one.

I hurried home, and my eldest sister, some twenty years my senior, had me clean, and then she cooked the doves with brown gravy for my dinner. I don't think I ever had a meal that was as tasty as those doves.

I had not gone to Point Lookout, but I had a successful hunting experience all by myself. I would see enough of Point Lookout in later years.

Sequel

Many years later, when my oldest son was twelve years old, he wanted a shotgun of his own. First, it was necessary to get him a hunting license, and he and I went to the courthouse in Leonardtown. As we entered the building, Mr. Benedict Greenwell, Chief Clerk of the Court of St. Mary's County, greeted us and began talking to my son. When he learned he was there to obtain a hunting license, he escorted him to the proper clerk. When the boy went to pay the cost, Mr. Greenwell took a dollar from his own wallet and said, "Let me have the honor of paying for your first hunting license." To this day, my son – will fondly recount this affair.

From the Courthouse, we proceeded to Dick Norris' hardware store on the village green. Here we purchased a single barrel 12 gauge Winchester shotgun. We told Mr. Norris about our encounter with the Clerk of the Court, Mr. Greenwell. Mr. Norris said, "Well, let me give this boy his first box of shotgun shells to go with the gun."

These two well-loved gentlemen are now gone but will never be forgotten by a certain father and son.

***

"There is no fury like an ex-wife searching for a new lover."
Cyril Connolly 1903 – 1974
***

Letter from St. Gabriel's Manor
by Fred McCoy
THE CHESAPEAKE

Chapter Thirty-Three

The Real Predators of the Chesapeake

By Cap'n Larry Jarboe

In the world's oceans, sharks are the apex predators of the watery realm that covers most of our planet.

Fortunately, there are few sharks compared to the multitude of fish species and other aquatic animals. Though we have done our best to disrupt nature through intense commercial fishing and man-made pollution, the world's oceans continue to seek natural balance despite our best efforts to the contrary.

The Chesapeake watershed is facing an onslaught of apex predators never seen in eons of evolution.

No, the Northern Snakehead fish from Asia is not nearly as great a threat to the eco-system as this new monster predator that was introduced by fishery biologists into the James River a couple decades ago.

The Blue Catfish is rapidly becoming the major threat to many of the estuarine species of migratory fish in the Chesapeake Bay tributaries. Already Blue Catfish represent up to seventy percent of the biomass of portions of the James River. Unlike the Great White Shark that lives a solitary existence, the Blue Cats prowl in large numbers, sometimes even thousands to the acre. These monster feeding machines have been recorded at over eighty pounds in the Potomac River and soon may reach over a hundred pounds for a single catfish as they have so grown in large Virginia lakes.

Even the dreaded snakehead fish is just another dinner entrée for a trophy size Blue Catfish.

This very lackluster season for Yellow Perch can easily be explained by the cold weather. However, growing pods of big Blue Cats in the Wicomico River and Nanjemoy Creek can easily swallow whole mature perch awaiting spawning season in the deep holes where they congregate before running upstream. Blue Catfish are opportunistic feeders that eat year-round despite cold weather conditions. What better to feeding ground than a cold deep hole full of lethargic perch to slurp down?

The Chesapeake ecosystem has been changed forever.

Don't expect the fishery managers to inform you of this simple fact. After all, they are the ones who imported the Blue Catfish from the Mid-West in the first place.

The good news is that Blue Catfish are easy to catch and excellent table fare.

Those of us who wish to put food on the table are fortunate to have a species that we can catch and eat with no limits.

Instead of spending hundreds of dollars to roam all over the Bay to catch and keep two Striped Bass, fishermen can easily hook a couple hundred pounds of big Blue Catfish from a small skiff close to shore. This is real meat fishing that also benefits the environment by removing invasive predators from the ecosystem that the fishery managers have so thoroughly disrupted.

There will always be a place for the charter boat that drags a couple dozen lines behind to catch a few Striped Bass. Also, the joy of catch and release bass fishing is a means of relaxation that many of us enjoy immensely.

But the very finest fishermen in the Chesapeake Bay watershed will be dragging hundreds of pounds in delicious Blue Cats out of their lairs for the very finest of fish fries.

The best way to beat them is to eat them. Bon appetite!

Cap'n Larry Jarboe – bass21292@yahoo.com

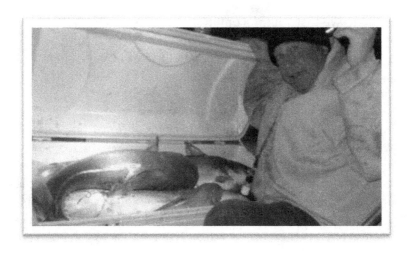

Chapter Thirty-Four

The Country Philosopher

To the County Treasurer:

By Stephen Gore Uhler

Congratulations, baby, you got yourself a nice little farm.

For years as you dug deeper and deeper into my assets, I resisted all thoughts of defeat. I considered you just another parasite to overcome. The other parasites, the hornworm, the Japanese beetle, all make their annual appearance to extract their levy on the product of my weary labors, so when your annual bill arrives, I just shrug my sweat-stained shoulders and accept the consequences.

I have always likened my condition to that of the little steam engine of childhood memory. "Puff, Puff, I think I Can, I Think I Can, and sure enough as each obstacle appeared on the horizon, I would puff and puff until I had surmounted it and then rest as I coasted downgrade.

I still have that youthful optimism in my mind, but alas, my work-worn old body refuses to cooperate. I arise each morning repeating the mantra of the little engine "I Think I Can, I Think I Can," but as sundown nears, I have to face reality, "I ain't gonna make it."

I must admit I like the format of this latest county tax bill. Most companies are sending out unreadable pages of computer printouts that leave the poor bill payer totally confused as to date due, amount due, and event to whom to send the money.

Your bill is so clear. It even has columns for the state share, the county share, and the fire departments share. You have spelled out the method for an annual payment, semi-annual payment. You have made it so easy. Except for one fact, it is never easy to get blood out of a turnip.

When I plod into Leonardtown in my threadbare, sweat-stained coveralls, wringing my callused hands, repeating over and over to myself that same old lie, "I Think I Can, I Think I Can," I cannot help noticing the hundreds of shiny new county vehicles parked around Leonard Hall.

And yet, when I call any county office on business, the person I need to speak with is "not available." Not that I really care. I expect to plod along until I join that big labor pool in the sky, but I worry that such a privileged class living high on the fruits of the laboring few could cause serious, systemic class envy.

We all know the history of the French Revolution. The downtrodden set up a few guillotines to remove some of the privileged officeholders, but when they found out how satisfying and efficient the zip-off guillotines were to them, they didn't stop until half of Paris was headless.

I knew I couldn't keep this existence forever. I just didn't think I would ever give it up to the tax collector. I always figured I'd lose the deed to this place in a card game or that some high stepping floozy would do a Samson and Delilah trick on me. I just never thought I would lose it by default to the tax collector.

But we all know what Robert Burns said about the best-laid plans of Men. Unfortunately, for me, I made my plans at a time in my life when I could work like a demon for 24 hours non-stop, take a few sips of spring water and be ready for another 24-hour stint.

Now alas, every little routine on this farm is a major chore. And money? There is no money.

Or what little money there is, is spent in the "golden triangle." I go to the first corner of the golden triangle – the doctor's office and then to Pharmacy, the second leg of the triangle, and then to the First National Bank for the last stop on the triangle. One look at what the drug bill has done to my bank balance, and I am ill again and have to rerun the triangle. Round and round I go like Alice down the rabbit hole, faster and faster-doctor, drugstore, bank, doctor, drugstore, and bank. I maintain equilibrium. The money is going out exactly at the rate it is coming in. Until "wham," I'm hit with my tax bill.

The game is over.

So Madame Treasurer, I want to bring you up to speed on what you will have to do on your new farm.

First, the dam on the pond which burst during hurricane Floyd, and which I have been trying to fix, will need to be repaired before M.D.E. finds out about the environmental damage to Hickory Landing Creek. If the State gets into the matter of the busted dam, you'll never be able to pay the bill.

Also, the sheep flock needs to be sheared (40 head x $8 = $320).

All of the horses need to see the blacksmith (12 x $20 = $240).

There are 3 raw colts that I have half broke but will need to be saddle broke as soon as my trainer gets out of Rappahannock jail in September. There is a lot of bush hogging that needs to be done before fall, which won't take long, but first, you will have to spend a couple hundred dollars for a new gearbox for the bush hog.

The two farm tractors are old but pretty reliable. The John Deere 820 needs a little clutch work, and the Ford 3000 probably needs a new alternator, but by-and-large, you got two nice tractors.

The John Deere dozer is in top shape except that it only steers on one side.

You can get a lot of work out of the dozer, but you must plan ahead and realize that all turns must be made to the right.

I have been postponing the application of lime and fertilizer until time got better, which looks like they ain't. Allow about $2,000 for lime and fertilizer.

I just had the barn roofs painted, and they look really nice, but there are some 6" x 6" sills that need to be replaced. The new sills I had sawn out 10 years ago are lying in the barn in good shape; you will need to hire the carpenter.

The Place is yours Ms. Tax Collector, lock, stock, and barrel, except for one 10' x 10' tarpaulin, which I will need to set up my residence on the courthouse lawn.

You may render me homeless, but by God, I will have my tent.

Chapter Thirty-Five

Officials Claim Crackdown on Outlaw Watermen; Fact or Myth?

By Ken Rossignol

(A continuing series focusing on Maryland's enforcement efforts on the Chesapeake Bay)

ANNAPOLIS, MD. --- For the past several years, Maryland has set out several initiatives designed to protect the native oyster species from over-harvesting and to grow the oyster beds, considered vital in that oyster's filter Bay water.

As part of that effort, large oyster sanctuaries have been established where oystering is either restricted or banned, making those areas tempting targets for one of Maryland's other native species --- the oyster pirate.

Oyster wars between Maryland and Virginia watermen raged for 150 years, and one group of Maryland oystermen who were raiding Virginia oyster beds were actually captured by a Virginia Governor who had organized a fleet of vessels to surround and fight the outlaws. Encounters between outlaw watermen and Maryland's Oyster Navy included violent gunfire directed towards the Oyster Police from the outlaws.

Historically, Maryland oyster pirates, whose descendants still believe that every fish, crab, clam, and oyster in the Bay belongs to them, have worked contrary to all rules of seasons and catch limits established by the governing authorities.

In contrast, the law-abiding and hard-working watermen who brave economic recession and the extremities of the weather to make a living, live within the rules. Ironically their tax dollars are employed to snare those who refuse to follow catch limits, seasons, and other restrictions.

The watermen have an organization to represent them in the Annapolis, but the leader of the group has a track record of being aligned with the oyster pirates more than of the hardworking group.

The State of Maryland and the Department of Natural Resources have harnessed all the methods of modern technology to catch the outlaw poaching Pirates of the Bay. Those methods include using State Police helicopters to track those tricky outlaws of the Bay, setting up radar and satellite technology, and using old-fashioned police work to snare those who wish to live life on the sly side.

Captured last November raiding an oyster sanctuary was William Cloyd Catlin Sr. and his brother Irving and in March of this year, William Catlin Sr. entered a guilty plea and was ordered to pay a fine of nearly a thousand dollars. As many watermen work with family members, they often poach with family members and employ the same habits of working around the rules.

One of the chief obstacles to levying fines of significance has been the relationship between States Attorneys and Judges in the counties which border the waterways and thus end up with citations and arrests being heard in the courts of those counties. Prosecutors and Judges have had long-standing friendships with many of the outlaw watermen, and a bushel of crabs or oysters often resulted in charges being dropped or low fines being assessed. Where bribery was not a factor, local prosecutors could often find a reason to toss a case, frustrating the DNR officers and making the watermen feel a great sense of bonding to the States Attorney in the next election.

As a result, the State of Maryland has now set up special dockets in the courts in most Maryland counties where a designated prosecutor will have a hard time dumping cases, and Judges will feel the spotlight. As a result, the first cases coming to trial this past year have seen significantly higher fines leveled at the transgressors.

The following is a look at the DNR and criminal records of William Cloyd Catlin Sr. and his son.

William Cloyd Catlin Jr DNR Citation History (DOB 07/07/1971)

Charged by Maryland State Trooper J. J. Resh with violating an ex-parte order on Nov. 1, 2004, the Somerset County States Attorney dropped the charge on March 11, 2005.

A warrant charging Catlin with being a fugitive from Justice in Ohio was served on March 24, 2008.

Charged by Crisfield Police Officer R. Taylor on Aug. 9, 2011, with driving while suspended. In Somerset County District Court on Sept. 9, 2011, States Attorney Daniel W. Powell dropped the charges. He was represented by the Assistant Public Defender in Princess Anne, whose salary is paid by the taxpayers. Between his arrest and the court date, Catlin was incarcerated.

Charged with a course of conduct of harassment and repeated

telephone misuse with repeated calls in Somerset County District Court, Catlin was found guilty of harassment in a plea deal with Somerset States Attorney Daniel W. Powell and fined zero dollars and sentenced to 90 days in jail with all of the jail time suspended. The telephone misuse charge was dropped.

Charged with assault for an incident that took place on May 4, 2012, the charges were dropped by the Somerset County States Attorney Daniel W. Powell (was appointed by Maryland Governor Larry Hogan as a Circuit Court Judge in 2017) on June 24, 2013.

Charged with possession of marijuana, paraphernalia and prescription narcotics which were not prescribed to him on Aug. 9, 2011, Catlin was represented by the Public Defender, who struck a deal with the Somerset County States Attorney Daniel W. Powell on Sept. 9, 2011 and Catlin entered a guilty plea to the pills and Powell dropped the other charges. As part of the deal, Catlin was sentenced to 12 months in jail with 10 months and 27 days suspended. He was incarcerated for the period between being arrested and the trial date and therefore credited with 33 days of time served.

Cited by DNR Officer Matt Corbin on Jan. 3, 2013, for possession over the limit of oysters. In Somerset County District Court, States Attorney Daniel W. Powell, Republican, dropped the charges on May 14, 2013.

Cited by DNR Officer Jeffrey Howard on Jan. 3, 2013, for possession of unculled oysters, Catlin went to trial in Somerset County District Court on March 29, 2013, where he entered a guilty plea and was fined $155.

Ordered by the Circuit Court Master Robert E. Laird on Nov. 12, 2013, in response to a child support warrant from the State of Ohio, to submit child support to the Child Support Administration.

William Cloyd Catlin Sr. (DOB Jan. 1949)
Upper Fairmount Md.

Cited by DNR Officer Cpl. Thomas Shores, on May 6, 1993, with crab scraping on leased oyster beds, Catlin Sr. pleaded guilty in Somerset County District Court on June 11, 1993, and was fined $70 and ordered to pay court costs of $20.

Cited by DNR Officer on Nov. 4, 1994, with possession of undersized oysters, Catlin Sr. pleaded guilty in Somerset County District Court on Dec. 2, 1994, and was fined $70 and court costs of $20.

Cited by DNR Officer Thomas Shores with failing to attend to a drift net, Catlin Sr. was given a probation before judgment on June 21, 1996, and paid no fine and was put on probation for one year.

Cited by DNR Officer T. Shores on Nov. 1, 2000, with possession of undersized oysters. In District Court for Somerset County on Dec. 1, 2000, he was found guilty and fined $70 plus court costs of $20.

Cited by DNR Officer V. Kulynycz on Aug. 17, 2004, with having his crab pots in a restricted area, Catlin Sr. entered a guilty plea on Sept. 9, 2004, and was fined $85.

Cited by DNR Officer J. W. Bromley IV on Nov. 25, 2013, with harvesting oysters from a sanctuary. In Somerset County District Court on March 3, 2014, he entered a plea of guilty and was found guilty by the Judge, who fined him $977.50 and ordered to pay court costs of $22.50. The court records do not reflect that he was represented by counsel.

This is one Judge who didn't get bribed with free oysters left on their back porch...

ANNAPOLIS, MD. — In the first major courtroom test of the Maryland Natural Resources Police's newest enforcement tool, two Somerset County watermen were found guilty Monday of harvesting oysters from a State sanctuary.

Officers used the Maritime Law Enforcement Information Network (MLEIN), a radar and camera system, on Nov. 25 to track a vessel moving in and out of the Somerset Sanctuary in Tangier Sound. They subsequently charged William Cloyde Catlin and Irving Lee Catlin with dredging in the protected area.

District Judge Paula Price ordered the vessel's captain, William Catlin, 64, of Upper Fairmount, to pay a $1,000 fine – $550 above the preset fine – and the mate, Irving Catlin, 55, of Westover, to pay a $450 fine. She gave them 30 days to appeal.

"When we launched our initiative in 2010 to restore Chesapeake Bay oysters, we included a tough conservation law enforcement component to protect this invaluable resource and let Marylanders know our commitment was rock solid," said Governor Martin O'Malley. "I'm pleased the court recognizes the importance of this effort."

After viewing images recorded by the MLEIN system, Judge Price ruled that despite the watermen's denials to the contrary, "it is clear to this court that you were in and out of the sanctuary, oystering."

"We are grateful to the court for accepting the use of MLEIN in our conservation law enforcement efforts and to Governor O'Malley for supporting the development of this system," said DNR Secretary

Joe Gill.

Judge Price noted that William Catlin has a history of crabbing, oystering and fishing violations dating back to 1982 and that Irving Catlin has natural resources convictions going back to 1979.

She dismissed the watermen's claims that it is sometimes difficult to stay outside the protected area and offered a suggestion: "If you're afraid of drifting into a sanctuary, then don't go anywhere near one."

The incident began shortly after 8 a.m. when an officer on land watched on his laptop as the Catlins crossed the boundary of the sanctuary, which is set aside by the State for oyster replenishment. The officer moved to his patrol boat to intercept them, all the while tracking their path on MLEIN.

During four passes inside the sanctuary, the watermen's boat motored in a circular pattern, indicative of an oyster dredging operation. The officer sped to the location as the workboat attempted to flee the sanctuary with its dredge still in the water.

NRP was able to retrieve the data from MLEIN that was used as evidence.

MLEIN, adapted from the Pentagon's geo-fencing initiative, became fully operational last fall. Each of the units in the network can cover up to 20 miles on the Chesapeake Bay, reaching from the mouth of the Susquehanna River to the Virginia state line.

"This is MLEIN's first full season on the Bay, acting as an extra set of eyes for our officers," said Col. George F. Johnson IV, NRP superintendent. "As we refine and expand its capabilities, and officers grow more comfortable working with it, we are confident the result will be more arrests and more convictions of poachers who steal Maryland's natural resources."

The Maryland Department of Natural Resources, the Office of the Attorney General, and the District Court of Maryland have expanded a successful program highlighting natural resources cases to 18 of Maryland's 24 jurisdictions. Under the program, cases including fishing, hunting, boating, and tree expert violations are heard on a specific day each month in the region where they occurred and prosecuted by a designated regional State's Attorney. NRP is working to have natural resource dockets put in place in the remaining six areas – Frederick, Harford, Montgomery, Prince George's, and Washington counties, and Baltimore City – by 2015.

Chapter Thirty-Six

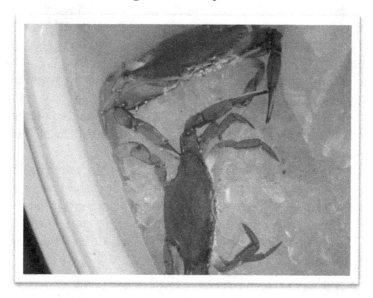

Crab Catching Techniques
Sure to Fill Your Basket

By A. Gail Whitney

"FIRST, ya have ta ketch 'em!"
That's what someone once told me. And I know just the places to go for the Chesapeake Bay blue crabs.

Before you go crabbing, you need some tackle for the tasty delights. People around the Bay crab in different ways. The simplest method is a crab net. Now for some places, you go like seawalls, or high piers to get those crabs, a short-handled net just won't do.

You can purchase long-handled nets at any tackle store or big box sporting goods store throughout the Chesapeake Bay region.

I personally don't like riding around with a long-handled net sticking out of the window of my car, so I have a break-down handle on my net. You can get the kind of that has a telescoping pole as well. I even make my own handles.

Drill a hole through each handle that you want to put together. Make the hole the size of the bolt you want you intend to use to fasten the two pieces together. Be sure to get the correct wing nut that fits the bolt when you are at the hardware store. If you have an extra-long pole, use two screws. The longer the extension, the harder the drag is on the net as it's pulled through the water and you don't want the pole to snap and lose your net, believe me, that will make you mad!

About the nets, as my husband always says, "Ya got your wire nets, and ya got yer string nets." I prefer the string nets. Every time I try to scoop up a crab, he crawls out of the firm wire net before I can flip him into the bucket. (Good crabbers can scoop and flip into a five-gallon bucket every time. They can! I've seen them do it.) I'd rather spend five minutes untangling a string net than catch a nice large male crab (a Jimmy) in a wire net and watch it plop back into the water to escape my pot. I use eels a lot as bait for crabs, and some people get irate to see me use their good-eating soft-shell crabs as bait. All you need is a ball of string to tie the bait and dangle in the water to attract the crabs. I've even used knitting yarn.

The day before I know I'm going crabbing, I take the chicken out of the freezer and punch a hole right through the bone of each piece. Then I use it to secure a string through the hole and around the chicken piece. Be sure to tie it and knot it a few times to make sure it's secure. Then I set it outside in an old varmint trap, so my cats don't eat it for lunch. By the time I get home from work, and it's time to go crabbing, my bait is pretty well cured and stinking real bad. I usually fix up four or five lines because everybody and his brother seem to figure out when I'm going crabbing and likes to tag along. But that's okay as the more crab catchers involved will add more crabs to the pot we will steam. We will reap our reward at the end of the day.

How to steam your crabs:

Pour about two inches of water in the bottom of your crab steamer, the kind with a rack in the bottom. Add one cup of vinegar and one beer. Add a half cup of Old Bay or another seafood seasoning to the bottom and bring your covered crab steamer to a full boil. Then it's time to use a big pair of tongs to place your crabs in the pot, taking time occasionally to gently give them a healthy covering of Old Bay in layers. Fill the pot and cover it and let it steam for about thirty minutes. You likely will have dropped a couple of crabs on the kitchen floor or had one scamper across the stove, so be quick about latching onto them with the tongs and toss them in with the rest of the bunch. Remember, it's important to have a rack in your pot as the idea here is to steam your crabs, not boil them. Steaming them to bright red color is the way to go.

Many folks like to have a cup of vinegar and a cup of seafood seasoning on your newspaper-covered table for dipping. If you don't have a crab mallet for cracking open legs, a knife handle will do fine.

If someone in your group doesn't know how to open and pick a crab, please don't show them. This is called conservation of an important resource of the Chesapeake. And that will make more for you to enjoy.

Crab pickers at work on banks of Chesapeake Bay.

Chapter Thirty-Seven

Races in Solomon's; Have they Gone Forever?

Growing up in Solomon's
By Pepper Langley

What I am speaking of are the last outboard races the faster inboard Hydroplanes that were so exciting to watch on the waterfront in Solomon's.

After WWII was over, I had a good friend of mine who had just come from the South Pacific and came over to see me. My friend's name was Preston Woodburn; his father owned Woodburn's Restaurant, where Pier I is located today. We had a long talk about the old times, and we both got very interested in outboard racing. Well, we both decided to get racing outboards, and he got the agency for the Speedliner hulls, which were fast boats and running in the runabout class D with 40 h.p. Mercury motors.

That fit just fine with our desire to race, but then there became so many who had the same idea that we soon had an outboard club organized at Solomon's. We had in the club about 28 racing members and all owned boats. That meant that every time we had a race, they all showed up and guaranteed a large race and lots of fun.

One of our well-known members was Mr. Carl Breland. He was considered the fastest driver as he was driving a Class C racer burning an alcohol mixture, and these were very fast racers and running around 80 mph.

I only raced outboards for two years, and then both Woodburn and I went to inboard racers. The first inboard racers we built were 135 cubic inches using 60 h.p. Ford V8 motors. They were fast boats, but when you are racing, you have the urge for more speed. So, Woodburn asked me if I would build him a 266 cubic inch Hydro, which I did. The boat was named the Thunderbird, and that put us in a class of boats running over 100 miles per hour. That was enough for us as, and we quit at that point as they were getting too fast.

Solomon's was well-known for their races and brought many people from all over the country, but soon it got to be the

Solomon's Island Yacht Club. They could not afford the races and gave up their sanction in the America Power Boat Association. From then on, the races were over at Solomon's Island.

What I would like to see is the return of the big races at Solomons and bring back the old gang, even if they can't race, they can meet old friends and talk about the old times on the waterfront at Solomon's.

(Editor's Note: Pier I is now Stoney's)

Chapter Thirty-Eight

Pirate Poachers of the Chesapeake:

Prosecutor Calls for Mandatory Jail Time for Repeat Offender Outlaw Watermen

By Ken Rossignol

PRINCESS ANNE, MD. --- The years of easy treatment in court for wayward and outlaw watermen – who truly believe themselves to be sacred cows – might be coming to a halt. At least those days are over for poachers and pirates of the Chesapeake, who end up on the docket of Somerset County States Attorney Dan Powell.

Powell, a native Somerset County lawyer, has been States Attorney since first winning the post in 2010, prides himself on honest work. He knows the hard-working watermen of his county do too and as difficult as changing regulations can be to adhere to, he knows that most of the region's watermen are following the rules regarding the catch of Chesapeake Bay fish, crabs, and oysters.

For a few scofflaws who have been banking on the easy treatment seen in some of Maryland's District Courts in past years, such as Lance Fridley and others soon to appear in Somerset County District Court, they might want to double down and hire a high-priced attorney. They are going to need them.

"I believe it's time the legislature enacts statutes calling for incarceration and mandatory penalties for repeat offenders," said Powell. "We have seen those changes in laws regarding other offenses, and the time has come to put real teeth into the law."

Powell has several cases coming up soon on his docket in Somerset County in which outlaw watermen are being cited for various offenses.

Natural Resources Police report that on Monday, Dec. 29, 2014, DNR officers set up surveillance near Deal Island in Somerset County to check for oyster harvesting before legal hours. At about 5:30 a.m., they saw a boat operating without navigational lights head into Tangier Sound.

DNR Police says that the officers tailed the vessel and watched its activity with night-vision glasses. Two officers boarded the vessel and directed the operator, Lance Carl Fridley, 29, of 10915 Tangier Acre Drive, Deal Island, to return to shore. Once back at Deal Island, the officers found seven bushels of oysters aboard his vessel, all containing oysters ranging from 55 percent to 69 percent of unsorted bivalves.

While honest and hardworking watermen follow the law and sort and cull their oysters at the point of catching them, returning the shells and undersized oysters to the bottom to grow and replenish, Fridley was simply keeping all he gathered.

Fridley was charged with seven counts of possessing unculled oysters, oystering before legal hours, having oysters aboard between two hours after sunset and sunrise, power dredging in a prohibited area, operating a vessel without navigational lights, and negligent operation of a vessel.

Prosecutor sets the record straight on Fridley

"The two cases where Mr. Fridley was incarcerated for theft and violation of probation (five months jail time) I was the State's Attorney, who prosecuted him. I am well aware of Mr. Fridley, and I am personally handling his case with Deputies Shores and Stanley in District Court on February 17, 2015. Case No. 5G18079 Mr. Fridley received 90 days in jail; Case No. 3G17559 Mr. Fridley received 90 days in jail. As to the theft case and assault cases that were NP while I have been State's Attorney, the victim in both cases who were the state's sole witnesses did not want to testify and asked my office to drop the cases. The other Assault case while I was State's Attorney was trie, and the Court found Mr. Fridley not guilty."

Powell checked case files for the earlier charges, which were dropped, and the files reveal that they were dropped by his predecessor.

Powell admits that the prosecution of poachers and outlaw watermen has not in the past been as strenuous as it perhaps should have been.

With four full-time attorneys and two part-time to handle the caseload, the rocket-docket of District Court, where hundreds of cases zoom in front of a District Court judge in a few hours at times, leaves justice seeping through the cracks.

Between the changing and shifting tides of the Bay, are new regulations of oystering setting aside areas of river bottoms designated as oyster sanctuaries.

The days of huge harvests of "white gold" as oysters were called in the 1800s now has turned boomtowns like Crisfield into ghost towns. The biggest deal in Crisfield is hauling tourists out to Smith and Tangier Islands. A sprawling marina filled with luxury boats is surrounded with tall iron fences to barricade out the thieves living in the nearby Section 8 housing complex.

Watermen are at odds with sport fishermen who love the return of trophy rockfish, which were almost fished to extinction until a moratorium was enacted in 1992.

Now the Rockfish are back in huge numbers.

Many watermen say that the explosion of the rockfish population is the cause of the low numbers for crabs. They say that when you clean your rockfish, you will find they are full of crabs.

Viewpoints of watermen towards the state-designated efforts range from supportive to hostile, with some calling the sanctuaries "oyster cemeteries" as a place where oysters are left to die.

The sport fishermen say that the watermen will steal the last oyster if they are allowed.

The watermen's association has had plenty of time to add the viewpoints of its members as laws have been regurgitated out of the legislative process in Annapolis. Between breakfast meetings to barroom late-night discussions in the taverns of the state's capital during the General Assembly sessions, the watermen have made their points to lawmakers.

Among the leaders of the watermen are some who have repeatedly been cited for violations and even one who bribed a Maryland DNR Police captain. That kind of background blends in well with the various criminal chicanery that the legislators have been known for from year to year.

The days of oysters and crabs by the bushel showing up on the back porch of judges and prosecutors may not yet be over, but with the public using their computers to track news stories in THE CHESAPEAKE TODAY, with some stories having had over 100,000 page views, less bartered bushels will likely appear in the future.

In short, the public is paying attention, and time will tell if the

Judges will pay attention to the public. District Court judges do not have to face the voters. They are appointed to ten-year terms and can retire at age 70 with full salary as their pensions. They often are haughty, arrogant, and aloof. They do as they damn please and answer really to no one.

The attitudes and expressions of the public on the Facebook page of THE CHESAPEAKE TODAY are vigorous, to say the least, with many of the posters – all of whom are self-identified – calling for strict penalties and large fines, confiscation of boats and equipment and lifetime banishment from the water for repeat offenders.

The decision over whether to prosecute belongs exclusively to the elected States Attorney of each county. He or she owes no one an explanation as to why charges are dropped or what kind of plea deal was made. No one but the voters.

The prosecutor is in the best position to bring about adherence to the law by insisting on a "pound of flesh" that means something instead of light or even non-existent fines as recently allowed by Talbot County States Attorney Scott Patterson who let two outlaw watermen off "Scott-Free."

Powell knows how he got his job. He has worked for it and calls it the best job he could ever hope to have and wants to keep it, and likely will.

After being appointed to West Point at the age of 17, he realized at the end of his second year that he truly wanted to be a lawyer and not a soldier. As it turned out, he left West Point, went to Salisbury and to law school, and along the way joined the Army Reserve and became both a lawyer and a soldier.

A key part of the process of how he landed his first job had nothing to do with the law or being a soldier.

When he interviewed with Baltimore County States Attorney Sandra O'Conner, he believes the fact that he lettered in softball in high school and the Baltimore States Attorney softball team needed some depth in right field made a difference. He got the job after O'Conner called Somerset County States Attorney Logan Widdowson for a reference; and ended up getting the girl too, as that is where he met his wife, Christine. While she was a prosecutor then, she now works on the 'dark side' as a public defender in Snow Hill.

Mixed in with the fishing violations of some of the outlaw watermen are criminal backgrounds ranging from burglary to drug dealing, with assault and domestic violence scattered through the criminal histories of many of them.

The near-epidemic of heroin and other drugs have Powell really worried.

"They try to say that marijuana is a harmless drug," said Powell. "That really isn't so, as criminals with guns often are selling weed or want to rob the ones who do."

Powell pointed over his shoulder, out of his office window to the main street of Princess Anne.

"Down that street there, one block, to the light and down the next corner is where a young fellow was standing there selling weed," said Powell. "A young man decided to rob him of his weed, and this seventeen-year-old kid fired his gun and killed the other young man, right here in the center of town and only over marijuana. No one can say that marijuana is victimless."

Powell also pointed to the influence that the Eastern Correctional Institution (ECI) has had in Somerset County.

"We got a lot of jobs from it, but there were other consequences as well," said Powell.

A recent article in a Salisbury website made a strong point that the citing of the prison in nearby Somerset turned Salisbury into a cesspool of crime. The point made by the editor of the SBY is that criminals move their families to the low-rent areas of Salisbury and ghettoize sections of the once-bustling city. Also, the point was made that inmates are released into the community instead of being shipped back to Baltimore, where most of them hail from. The article argued that Salisbury is being turned into a crime-ridden haven for Baltimore's vermin and that local officials are clueless, and some are profiting from the spread of low-rent housing development.

Powell was asked if prisoners are being released into Somerset County.

"I did look at records of the county during the two years when I was county administrator," said Powell. "I did see a letter from Governor Harry Hughes pledging that the state would not be releasing prisoners into Somerset County if the county would accept the prison. That is not the case any longer, they are released here."

With the busy U. S. 13 highway running parallel to Princess Anne and carrying with it all of the challenges of law enforcement of the modern society, the contrast to environmental challenges is mixed.

Who would ever have thought that outlaw watermen were also part-time burglars and drug dealers?

The Maryland State Police recently cracked open a case of

black drug dealer pimps running black hookers from Princess Anne to Pennsylvania and keeping them as slaves in a local motel room. One hundred and fifty years ago, blacks seeking freedom were spirited away from plantations in Somerset County north up the Delmarva Peninsula to freedom in Pennsylvania. That was the infamous 'Underground Railroad.'

Thus where once was the Underground Railroad to freedom for blacks escaping the slavery embraced by white plantation owners, now blacks are seen enslaving other blacks to make a buck, and U. S. Route 13 was the main drag for delivering hookers to customers?

Still, the system of justice is centered on each county's courthouse, and in Somerset, that is Princess Anne. The county has its District Court in a converted space in a shopping center, next to other offices that hand out welfare, in a virtual one-stop shopping of services to the revolving door of poverty and crime. The Circuit Courthouse stands in the center of the old town which, like other Maryland towns that had traffic bypass them, is filled with antique shops and lots of empty spaces.

The 1904 red-brick structure was built to reflect "The early Twentieth-century prosperity and the colonial heritage of Somerset," says the signpost in front of the courthouse. That is so, and so is the District Court, which is almost an annex of the welfare and social services office next to it, reflecting the poverty, drugs, and crime.

Princess Anne, like so many other towns, is struggling, but it is also fighting to move ahead. Signs of churches, events, parades, and activities to retain community spirit can be seen in windows and window dressing.

The University of Maryland Eastern Shore is on the other side of town from the busy north-south highway that funnels traffic from New York to Florida.

Also, running up the peninsula is the rail line that still serves freight traffic from Cape Charles north to Delaware.

With a state prison, a national highway, a large state college, and a tightening natural resource, Somerset County is in a perfect storm for all of the pressures of society to erupt into the courtrooms of Princess Anne.

Powell points to several murders his office has had to handle as well as infamous murder cases moved to Princess Anne as a change of venue.

The town may look like Mayberry on the outside, but to a large extent, the challenges are the same here as everywhere else.

The Town has a set of commissioners, one of whom recently entered an 'Alford Plea' to charges of assault. Town Commissioner Lionel Frederick was charged with spraying a cohort with mace and striking the victim with his van. In a plea deal, he was given 100 hours of community service, and the motor vehicle rap was dropped by a Special Prosecutor.

The commotion of criminal charges for Commissioner Frederick was on the front page of the local newspaper. He posed for *The Daily Times* newspaper in front of a storefront church window with the words "Pure World Bible Church" prominently displayed as he appeared next to the window in his white suit and tie, and dreadlocks draped over his shoulders. Not exactly Marion Barry but not too far from it.

But the juxtaposition of the store window to Frederick heading to court shows he has a great command of how to capture the media, if not the moment. Even small-town politicians have adoring media, just like President Obama in D.C.

The Town didn't have a way to bounce Frederick off the Town Council as apparently there are no standards to hold office. Just like the rest of America, in Princess Anne, the voters get to have who they want in office.

As H. L. Mencken said one hundred years ago, "The common man knows what he wants, and he deserves to get it, good and hard."

As politics and law go, Somerset seems to be well-served and has great diversity.

Longtime attorney, Democrat Delegate and now Circuit Court Judge Dan Long enjoy strong respect from many; a hard-working set of commissioners in Princess Anne led by Commissioner Dennis Williams is making headway, and Dan Powell shows that as a prosecutor, the hard-working Republican is doing what he has always done – work hard. Powell prides himself on having earned his own way through school and never piled up the burden of student loans. The son of a teacher and a farmer, Powell, learned early in life that working for a living provided value and purpose to everyone in a community.

Powell said he learned in school, the military, and working as a prosecutor and county administrator on how to be a leader. He says he looks forward every day to coming to work and getting a chance to provide leadership.

Many in Somerset believe he is doing just that.

As Princess Anne Commissioner Williams said of Powell, "we all love Danny a lot, he does a great job for the county."

Synopsis of Fridley's record:

∘Fridley was charged with a bevy of traffic charges after a crash on Sept. 1, 2014, at Rollan Parks Road and Deal Island Road in which he was also cited for DWI by Somerset County Sheriff's Deputy A. Stanley. His trial on those charges is set for Feb. 17, 2015.

∘On July 12, 2014, Fridley was charged with theft, and States Attorney Dan Powell dropped the charges.

∘On Oct. 24, 2014, Fridley was charged with possession of 145 unculled oysters by DNR Officer Brimer and is due in court on Jan. 13, 2015, for that case. (Powell said that Fridley failed to appear in court for that date, and a warrant will likely be issued for his arrest.)

∘On Jan. 15, 2011, charges of second-degree assault against Fridley were dumped by the Somerset County States Attorney Dan Powell. Fridley was represented by a Public Defender courtesy of the taxpayers. (See Powell explanation above that the victim didn't want to testify and requested that the charges be dropped.)

∘On Sept. 12, 2011, Fridley was charged with assault in Somerset County District Court. In a plea deal with the Somerset County States Attorney, Fridley entered a guilty plea and paid no fine, did no time.

∘On July 23, 2009, Fridley was charged in Somerset County Circuit Court with drug distribution charges. The prosecutors often allow dumping charges when the culprit rats on his competitors in the drug trade. On Aug. 11, 2009, Kristy Hickman, the States Attorney for Somerset County, put all the charges on the Stet Docket. Fridley paid no fine, did no time, and the Judge waived the court costs.

∘On April 26, 2009, Fridley was charged with assault, and Somerset County States Attorney Hickman put the case on the Stet Docket, with no fine, no time.

∘On Jan. 14, 2005, Fridley was charged with theft, and on Sept. 27, 2005, Kristy Hickman, States Attorney for Somerset County, put the charges on the Stet Docket with no fine and no time. The taxpayers funded his legal representation from Public Defenders (now District Court Judge in Wicomico County) John Rue and Bruce C. Anderson.

Chapter Thirty-Nine

The Country Philosopher

Born on the wrong side of the blanket

By Stephen Gore Uhler

Scientists had decoded the human D.N.A. When I was studying biology many, many years ago, there were some pretty good theories about genes and chromosomes. Our teachers could mathematically predict who would have a brown-eyed child and how many cattle in a herd would have white faces. We learned about dominant and recessive genes and why mules can't produce offspring. Genetic outcomes could be generally predicted, but there was much that could be done about it.

Now with gene splicing, we will be able to construct the perfect human specimen.

Have you always hated your buck teeth and cross eyes? Do you want to spare your children all of those hours at the orthodontist? Simple. You just cut those bad genes out of your DNA and splice in someone else's.

If you are about to choose your mate, don't waste a lot of money on candy and flowers until she has produced a printout of her DNA. If it looks like she is going to require a lot of expensive gene splicing to produce the quality of offspring that you desire, pass her up. There are better fish in the sea.

The eugenics proposed by Adolf Hitler and Dr. Mengele was rather haphazard. Even by their selective breeding, there was a lot left to chance.

I have been a breeder just about all of my life. I am not referring to my reputation as a "skirt chaser," I mean, plants and animals.

Long before I heard of Gregor Mendel and his wrinkled peas, my elder farmers were passing on to me the importance of selective breeding.

Grandpa would walk his tobacco rows for hours until he found the perfect plant that would be selected to produce the seed for the next season's crop. You had to get to your plant before the flowers opened, and the hummingbirds came. Hummingbirds love tobacco nectar, and they move so fast. There were about 7,000 tobacco plants per acre. I have watched those little ruby-throated lechers buzz up and down the rows hitting every blossom with their beaks covered with pollen from God knows where. If you wanted perfect tobacco to market every year, you had to protect the breed and save the seed.

Some of the varieties of tobacco had been bred and refined for so many years. The seed was sold under the family name. You had such varieties as "Moore," "Robinson," "Catterton," and my favorite, "Shakespeare Bowling."

After the University of Maryland got into the plant breeding business, the breed was identified by number, "Md 57" "609".

The numbered breeds from the University scientists were actually better specimens than "Shakespeare Bowling," but I don't think that those serial numbers had the romance of those old family names.

Saving seed corn was by the same process. By the time I knew my grandfather, his old bones were stiff and arthritic, just as mine is today. I would run ahead of him and select plants that, to my young eyes, were perfect, but his wise old eyes would find something wrong with them - "roots too weak," "years don't hang a right," "stalks not strong enough."

Grandpa didn't allow himself many "cuss words," especially in the presence of children or women. His favorite epithet was "scalawag," which was a hold-over from the days when the hated blue coats rode through Southern Maryland, burning the barns and running off the farm help.

"Hup! Thunderation, you scalawag". I knew Grandpa was getting tired of my gallivanting and so I would quiet down for a while to let him forget my present transgressions, and then start up again.

Nowadays, you can just walk into the seed store and select the seed variety that you think will suit your needs, seeds that have been bred and crossbred by such international conglomerates such as Archer-Daniels-Midland or some such outfit. The seed stock from such an outfit is so specialized that today's farmer has to fertilize, irrigate and spray with insecticide and herbicide with mathematical precision.

Do the least thing wrong, and you've got no crop at all. Those old seeds the old-timers saved had to thrive on poor land, against wiregrass, bindweed, borers, blights, and droughts. Those old plants had to take a licking and keep on ticking. We didn't set production records back in the good old days, but a man with a few acres and a healthy mule could feed his family.

Breeding livestock was more direct. If the bull or stallion met with your approval and the moon and star were properly aligned, you would usually get what you bred for.

Back in the "good old days," before milk came in plastic jugs and butter came in plastic tubs labeled "spread," every family kept a cow or two for milk and butter.

The cows needed to be bred every year to "freshen" them and to yield a calf for sale or to keep as the occasion required.

My father was usually gone from the farm from dawn to dark working, and us boys tended to the farm (in our fashion). One morning he left instructions for us to put a rope on old "Bossy" and lead her to the nearest farm and have her bred.

Dr. Johnson's farm was right adjacent to ours, and he had a fine Jersey Bull, but that sucker was mean. Jersey Bulls, as a breed, are meaner than most, but Dr. Johnson's bull was a mean, evil, sum bitch. He would hurt you if he could. We boys decided that rather than lead our cow one mile to Dr. Johnson's farm and face almost certain mayhem, that we would walk her the three miles to Mr. Zack Fowler and use his young, gentle Guernsey Bull.

The Fowlers kept the store in Chaptico. Mrs. Fowler was postmistress while Mr. Zack kept the store, and I mean they kept a store, not like that "Chaptico Market" that Jackie Tennyson attempts to operate, but a real store with shoes and bolts, horse collars and soda crackers. Not quite as big as Mrs. Agnes Guy's store in Clements, but a real general store none-the-less.

We boys had it figured. We would get permission from Mr. Zack and then turn our cow in with his bull and enjoy our big Rock Creek while watching the bull's handiwork from the board fence.

We boys were 10-11 years old at the time and considered ourselves accomplished stockmen by that age. We led the old cow right up to the store porch, and Mrs. Fowler came out. "Where are you boys going with that cow?"

"She's in heat Mrs. Fowler, and we figured it would be o.k. to use your bull."

Mrs. Fowler had been a school teacher for years and had that certain stentorian voice that old schoolmarms practiced back in the "good old days."

"Zack! Zack! Come here, Zack, right away." The poor lady went into a swoon. She was of the old school where people didn't discuss animal breeding in the presence of ladies, especially innocent young children of 10-11 years.

We didn't know what all of the fuss was about. We were experienced young farmhands of 10-11 years, we were good neighbors to the Fowlers, our cow was in heat, and the Fowlers owned a willing bull. What else was there to talk about?

Mrs. Fowler came out of her swoon and went immediately into a Crimson blush, and then we thought she would swoon again.

Why didn't we just take the cow to Doctor Johnson's?

We wouldn't have had the big, ice-cold orange soda to drink, but we could have watched the bull as long as we wanted. Dr. Johnson would have been busy in his office and certainly wouldn't have been running around hollering and turning white, then red, and white again.

Mrs. Fowler finally composed herself and read the law to Mr. Zack. "Zack, I want you to tell those boys to take that animal home, and you need to talk to their father."

"To hell with that Prissy old school Marm, let's go to Dr. Johnson's."

We then had to walk four miles back to Dr. Johnson's, where we should have gone in the first place.

But, we could cut a mile off our walk by cutting through Long woods. Long woods was a scary walk through the woods with all kinds of ponds with big water snakes. It was a haven for bootleggers. Suppose old Bossy got a whiff of fermenting mash. You can't keep a cow out of a mash barrel once she gets a whiff of it. It wouldn't be no fun trying to drag a drunk cow two or three miles through the woods.

We lucked out and got past the water snakes, and didn't run up on nay "kittles." We were making a good time when we passed Mr. John Young's farm. Mr. John had a big job up in Washington, driving a cab or something, and only came down on Sundays. His fence was only about three rails high, and behind that fence was a nondescript mixture of cattle, including a juvenile half-Angus bull.

Our feet were getting tired, and sheep flies were eating the hell out of us.

The thought struck us all at once. "Let's give him a shot."

After all of that walking, "Old Bossy was in full estrus, she needed no coaxing. She cleared those three rails in one leap, and in less than a minute, we had a calf on the way.

That night our father came in. "You boys get that cow bred?"

"Yes, suh."

Nothing more was said until the following spring. When my father saw that lop-eared, black, a muley calf born to his fine Guernsey cow, he went off.

"Whose bull did you boys use?"

"Mr. John Young's."

"Damn worthless calf. You'd might as well knock it in the head."

Papa must not have been feeling well, we didn't even get an ass whipping.

"He just cussed under his breath about the "damn worthless calf."

But, for some reason, we kept that "damn worthless calf." We kept her for years. She turned out to be the best milker, gallons, and gallons of rich, creamy milk every day, and she was gentle; anybody could milk that cow.

She might have been born on the "wrong side of the **blanket," but she earned her keep for years.**

Chapter Forty

The Washington Post

1150 15ᵗʰ STREET, N. W

WASHINGTON, D. C. 20071

FAX NUMBER (202) 334-5075

BENJAMIN C. BRADLEE
VICE PRESIDENT At Large
(202) 334-7515

October 21, 1992

Mr. Kenneth C. Rossignol
St. Marys Today
P.O. Box 689
California, MD 20619

Dear Ken:

When I was an editor I hated to receive thank-you notes.
They made me feel that I had not been tough enough.

So this isn't a thank-you note.

Instead it's a letter of thanks for the help you have given
all of us involved with trying to bring that city up from
the ground with taste and intelligence.

See you soon,

Ben

The Joy Boys of the Washington Post Elevator

By Ken Rossignol

WASHINGTON, D.C. --- After Ben Bradlee bought a weekend farm in St. Mary's County, Md., he began subscribing to my newspaper, St. Mary's Today, and I called him to thank him for his business. He invited me to D.C. for lunch, and that began a twenty-five-year friendship where we often had lunch in Lexington Park or in Washington to talk about his leading the St. Mary's City Historical Commission or politics in general.

One day after having lunch at the Madison Hotel across from the Washington Post offices in Washington, Ben Bradlee and I were returning to his office and took the side door into the building and ran to catch an elevator as the door started to close.

In the elevator were legendary Post editorial cartoonist Herbert Block, known forever as Herblock, and Washington Post publisher Don Graham.

Bradlee introduced us, and then I asked, "Mr. Block, in your cartoons, are you the artist and the smart-ass or just the artist?"

"Why do you ask, Sonny," said Block.

"Well, in my newspaper, I hire an artist to draw the cartoon art, but I am the smart-ass with the idea in the toon as I understand the issues but haven't a clue as to how to draw."

With a loud laugh, Block answered: "Hell, I do it all, and those two SOBs there (pointing to Graham and Bradlee) are always trying to tell me what to put in a cartoon, but I just tell them to 'Go to Hell.'"

Graham and Bradlee agreed.

"That's what he always says," said Bradlee with a laugh, echoed by Graham.

In his Washington Post office, Editor Ben Bradlee reviews an article about Christopher Columbus in that day's edition with Ken Rossignol. Bradlee, a subscriber to Rossignol's newspaper, ST. MARY'S TODAY, had his issue of the weekly paper, shown on his desk, delivered to him that week by the Publisher instead of in the mail.

Photo by Patrick Pena.

Chapter Forty-One

Stormy Day at Solomon's Island

By Mark Robbins

The best place for sailing that ever was is the Chesapeake Bay. I don't mean only that it is big with thousands of miles of coastline, dozens of navigable rivers, may hundreds of navigable creeks with literally thousands of quiet, beautiful places to anchor and enjoy nature.

For me, the most fascinating aspect of sailing the Bay is the people you meet. There is a spirit of community among sailors on the Bay. For example, the time I was all stormed in and tuckered out at Solomon's Island.

If it had not been for a complete stranger coming to my aid at the just the right moment, I might as well have had a full-fledged disaster on my hands.

My problems started when I accidentally left my second anchor and rode at my marina when I left in November on my last cruise of the year. Therefore, I didn't have them when my 30-foot sloop Baraka and I were caught in heavy weather. When the heavy weather struck, I was near the midpoint of the Choptank and Patuxent Rivers. Despite headwinds, I altered course, under storm sail only, for the Patuxent River. The seas grew larger, the wind freshened. Just standing up at the helm of the rolling and pitching,

Baraka drained a man's stamina.

The wind veered to the north-northeast as I arrived dog tired at Spring Cove Marina in Back Creek. All I wanted to do was drop anchor and make some hot cocoa and maybe sleep.

The first attempt to anchor was a near disaster. The flukes of the 25 pound Danforth anchor became so fouled in a length of half-inch cable preventing the anchor from biting into the bottom. At this moment, the auxiliary diesel stalled. Baraka began dragging its useless anchor toward the docks of Cove Point Marina.

The situation would have been desperate except this time, for the first time ever, I had a bolt cutter on board. For years, I had put off buying this standard item for sailors. Bolt cutters are important after being dismasted to cut away the stainless steel rigging to prevent its fouling the propeller. Bolt cutters can save your life if you are dismasted in heavy weather.

I never did buy a bolt cutter.

Providentially, I won one in a church raffle on the Eastern Shore several days before my arrival at Spring Cove.

Divine intervention seemed possible because I attended my first church raffle by accident, and I bought a ticket only to be polite, and I won the needed bolt cutter. If it wasn't divine intervention, it was an awful lucky coincidence.

The bolt cutter easily cut away the cable freeing the flukes of the Danforth anchor. The boat drifted dangerously close to the slipped sailboats before I could restart the engine. Not wanting to foul the anchor again on the cable at Spring Cove, I anchored near the center of the anchorage between the Calvert Marine Museum and Zahnhiser's Marina. There were no other boats anchored there, so I would enjoy the advantage of a large scope.

I veered out all 150 feet of my anchor rode, which gave me a scope of about 15, but this was not enough. Almost immediately, the catenary flattened, the anchor rode snubbed, the chocks bit savagely into the chafing guards. Every time the anchor rode snubbed, the sloop shuttered, rattling everything aboard that could rattle. The violent motion was dangerous and raised the possibility that the anchor rode would chafe through the chocks. It's awful to face problems like this when you are falling down tired.

Because there was no more anchor rode onboard, the only hope of stopping the snubbing was to increase the catenary between the bow and the anchor. To do this, I jury-rigged a sentinel by shackling the heavy bolt cutter, and a twenty-pound anvil to the anchor rode.

The sentinel (anchor weight) was slipped down the anchor rode. A 75-foot length of stout cord assured the sentinel's descent to midway between the anchor and the bow. The snubbing stopped. The gentler motion of the boat made staying awake more difficult, and it was essential that I remain awake and as alert as possible. My growing fatigue was becoming as big a problem as the raging storm.

The wind shrieking in the standing rigging pierced the eardrums. Earplugs could not noticeably dampen the shrieks. But the shrieks served a useful purpose; they would keep you awake for a while, and that was of the first importance until the wind subsided.

At this moment from the lee shore, a bearded man wearing yellow foul weather gear signaled with his hands to remove the dinghy from the bow and let it drift to him on the lee shore. This would reduce windage and snubbing. With sign language, the man on shore seemed to indicate he would bring the dinghy back when the wind let up. He was a kind burly sailor, and he helped me when I needed it the most.

With the dinghy now safely ashore, the wind had much less to bite on, and the sloop rode the anchor better than before. I could relax a little now, but it would be unwise to sleep; too much could still go wrong. I was indescribably tired. God! I wished I had someone on board to spell me. I was angry at myself for having left my plough anchor back at my marina. With two anchors, I would have anchored securely enough to get at least a little sleep. I set the alarm clock to ring in thirty minutes then placed it safely out of reach.

I could feel my fatigue gaining on me, so I forced myself to think of something that would keep me awake. It was a final desperate effort to stay awake. I thought of having the diesel auxiliary, the galley stove and the heater all work off diesel fuel.

I found the thought amusing and laughed a tired laugh, but now I wondered where I could put the Charley Noble to take away fumes from the galley and heater. The head was too small. The forward cabin was a possibility, but a lot of heat-proof insulation would be necessary to prevent anyone from using the bunk from being burned. Maybe I could use the Charley Noble straight up through the overhead. This would come out near the mast where it would interfere with handling the mainsail. I knew there must be a place for the Charley Noble, but my fatigued mind could not think of it.

Whimsically, I thought I could combine the Charley Noble with a periscope I would not have to go topside so frequently because I could survey the situation outside the boat through the periscope without having to go outside. I was pleased to think that perhaps I was the first person on the planet to have that thought. To me, at that moment, it was hilarious to think that if the U. S. of A. could get a man on the moon, that surely, someone in the Republic could get a charlie noble combined with a periscope, but then, who besides me would be interested. I thought and moved sluggishly. All this whimsical and irrational thinking and empty laughter meant, that, of course, I was losing my battle with fatigue.

The alarm clock rang, indicating it was time to go topside and see what was happening. On deck, I found the sentinel was working well. Gusts of wind would blow the boat toward the lee shore, the catenary would flatten, and the sentinel would tug the anchor rode down toward the bottom, thereby increasing the catenary and the holding power of the anchor. The boat was riding as well as could be expected in heavy weather.

Then I saw that my dinghy was no longer on the lee shore where the bearded sailor had put it. Instead, the dinghy and the bearded sailor were now approaching rapidly from upwind. It was unnecessary to row. The sailor only used the oars to guide the dinghy as the wind pushed it.

He must have trucked the dinghy around to a point upwind to make the approach easier and faster. I was so tired it was difficult to stand, and I thought I was seeing things. But the big, bearded sailor was no illusion. He came aboard over the stern pulpit. I think he told me his name, but I was too tired to remember it. He said I looked like I could use some rest and that he would look after the boat for a while.

I made a thermos bottle of black coffee for him and crawled into my bunk. I slept the kind of sleep you only have when you are so tired you can no longer think, and your arms and legs feel like blocks of lead. Much later, I woke because the boat had stopped its rhythmic motion against the wind and waves. The sea was calm now. The sun was shining. I was alone!

I found an unsigned note that all was well aboard the Baraka and recommended that I buy a second anchor. Someone had fetched the bearded sailor from the boat. He knew it was safe for me to continue to sleep. I was dangerously fatigued and needed sleep. Still, I wish I had been able to thank him properly. My debt to him is great because at the time he came aboard, I was too tired to have responded effectively to any kind of emergency.

I do not know how he could tell from the distance of the shore that I was so tired, but he did, and he came to help me. He didn't wait to be thanked, and I have not seen him since. I hope someday to have a chance to repay him. I owe him.

Sailing on a fair day on Patapsco River. *THE CHESAPEAKE TODAY photo*

Chapter Forty-Two

Lenny's latest serving

By Lenny Rudow

There's been many a day I can remember spending chasing the King of the Bay, the granddaddy of 'em all, the sacred Solomon's Island Super Striper.

Now, Y'all know I wouldn't tell ya a word that wasn't the honest fact of the matter and direct to the point. But I gotta remind you that afore I tell this yarn, I ain't speaking 'bout any 'old tale – this un's the truth and nothing but the truth!

There was day years and years back when I was jest a young' un' that I overheard the charter boat captains speakin' to one another back at the dock.

I was trappin' minnies on the dock, and through their hushed tones, I knew they were speaking' of something serious, but they didn't pay me no mind. They were all listening to one captain who was warning them – that there was a new danger in the Bay. He had brought his boat back to the dock with a hole in the hull the size of Colorado, and he swore, and I believe him to this day, it was done by the biggest, meanest, most powerful Rockfish ever to live.

Tough the years I had heard many tales about the Solomon's Super Sacred Striper. I was never sure he existed, though. After time had passed, my memory faded, and I forgot about the stories I'd heard and overheard. That is, until last week. I was driftin' for trout 'n Flounder in the River, just a mile or so from the island when I felt a hit on my line that rattled my berries. My reel 'n rod nearly got pulled from my hands, and the line was peeling off my reel. Well, now, that fish didn't waste a moment's time – he kept running' til the last of the line was out of my reel. Then turned and headed right for my boat!

When the fish turned, his tail created a whirlpool so big it sucked in thirty sailboats! He smashed my boat right under the water line and kept pushing' til half his head was inside the cabin of my boat. Then he opened up wide, and sucked every last crumb of food and bait outta my cooler in the galley.

I limped back to shore safely, taking on the water the whole time. Like I said, now all this is the plain truth. Jest wanted to warn ya'll.

Chapter Forty-Three

The Sea, The Boat, and I

By Vi Englund

It is 0100, 10 May 1972. It's a rough day approaching the Gulf Stream. Most of this trip has been normal. Even this last part has been normal.

We are in pitching head seas. Below deck is in shambles. Dan's black hair protrudes from beneath a blanket. Al's nose is fiery red. Perhaps he dreams of his wife, his three-week-old daughter, and dogwood blossoms in Maryland.

Randy, at the helm, seems to have forgotten his newly minted degree from San Diego State.

The skipper sleeps in the aft cabin. For the second day in a row, he missed a noon sight because of overcast skies.

I, with my monel stomach, am pressure cooking a chicken, sipping hot buttered rum, and contemplating this mess. Why go to sea on a sailboat?

On one voyage, I decided I went to sea for the good days. Just me on a ship, with a scrap of muslin on a flat sea. Now, I'm not so sure. Maybe it's for the bad days.

The wind quickened. We took a big one over the bow. A slight groan from the helmsman. The pressure cooker hissed a bit of extra steam, as the gimballed stove did its thing. That chicken smells mighty fine. Al turned slightly green about the mouth and pulled the blanket over his head. I lock my legs about the table support and continue to write.

About those bad days.

Yesterday, in rising winds and heavy seas, we furled the main. Everyone did his job, nothing went wrong, and the main lay tucked securely. The crew allowed themselves a few moments of elation and then fell into almost dry bunks. Randy stood the watch. He took a big beam sea, water splashed over his drawn face, and he looked just plain pitiful.

I said I'd take the wheel.

First, I brought him a hot water bottle. This not only brings warmth to the irritated stomach but gives the seasick one a feeling of being loved – if it's only by a hot water bottle.

He tucked the warm bottle under his slicker, curled up on the cockpit seat. He grinned weakly and said, "If you keep it up north a bit, maybe we won't get washed overboard."

He didn't act as though he really cared.

At the wheel, that one hour made this particular voyage worth it. I forgot all the aggravation of being beat. That one hour, more life surged through me than on a multitude of just plain days, or even good days at sea.

The sea's like rolling mountains swept toward *Coppra's* beam. It because of a joyous game to outwit them. And I laughed if I won, I laughed it I lost. For it was a game. Though the stakes were high, there was nothing personal on either side.

How can I describe that hour? I looked to the west. At the farthest distance, I saw a high white mountain – like a snow-capped peak on the rim of vision. I gasped. My knees chilled. My stomach froze. Not in fear, but in awe of seeing such a sight. Though high noon, the sky darkened with low fast-moving clouds. A wave lifted. Before it broke, the top glowed a color – a color between jade and turquoise, translucent as a gem. The same brilliant hue lay in the troughs.

How high the waves? Who really can measure a wave? Thirty feet. How strong the wind? The skipper said forty, with gusts of fifty. *Coppra* leaped ahead as though she too felt joy at this moment. Of doing what she was designed and built to do. A harmony of joy at this moment. The sea, the boat, and I.

So why do you do it? Do anything. Fall in love, tend a marriage, raise a family, work in a profession, raise a garden, play a sport, strive to achieve, pursue an art, a loved one – or life itself.

I sailed. I saw a sight through these eyes. Heard the roar of the pounding seas and the howl in the rigging. I smelled the spray, tasted the salt, felt the vessel speak its language. All were recorded in my mind. A sight that no one else saw at this moment in time.

It is strange, so much is happening out here. And even stranger there is someone to see it.

But that was yesterday. Today, I sit at the table and try to recapture it.

Making an ocean passage has many facets. Usually, at some point on the voyage, one experiences a moment of insight. For a man meets himself at sea. It brings out the worst in a man, it brings out the best. Life does the same thing ashore, but it is more subtle. The process of learning seems to speed up at sea. If you tremble to know yourself, stay away from the sea. Keep your gaze attached to soil, trees, grasslands, hills, and mountains. Fasten your sight upon the freeways, the stoplights, and the buildings. Never glance skyward. For if you study the horizon, it will one day lead to the seashore. The necklace of foam left by the waves on the beach will tempt you on – on to the place where you will meet yourself. Just you and the ocean deeps.

Chapter Forty-Four

Tick's Last Laugh

Baseball and Early Days
By Lou Clements

An outstanding baseball player was Al "Tick" Gough Sr., of Leonardtown, Maryland. Tick was Leonardtown's star player, a hard-throwing right-hander, who could hum that old ball. He pitched every Sunday and lost very few games. Tick was a firm believer in practicing. Bill Redmond, Tick, and I would meet at the North End and on the sidewalk by Mary Miles and warm-up Tick. He could throw for hours and never seem to be tired. This one day with Bill catching, Tick cut loose with a fastball down low, the ball hit Bill on his toe, bounced once on the sidewalk, and hit a basket of clothes a woman was carrying on her head. Clothes went everywhere! When Bill removed his shoe, his big toenail popped off.

Al "Tick" Gough was Leonardtown's ace pitcher and was a constant winner. I only saw him knocked out of the box once, on a hot July 4th, 1932. The Washington Red Sox came to town. Tick had defeated them 4-3 on their last trip to Leonardtown. On this particular day, Tick marched up on the pitcher's mound, rubbed up the baseball, threw his warm-up pitches, stepped back on the rubber, reared back, and cut loose with his fastball. The ball never reached Al Snyder's catcher's mitt. With a hefty swing by the batter, the ball went sailing into another county.

Tick, surprised, hitched up his pants, pulled down on his cap, stepped again on the rubber, and fired his best pitch. With a vicious cut by the batter, Tick watched the ball go sailing out the ballpark. This went on all day. Tick kept firing away, and the Red Sox kept coming back with hits. Leonardtown, having a great defensive team, was able to keep the score respectable at 9-2, but still a major loss.

After the game, we found out this was a hand-picked team from the Washington Industrial League, one of the best semi-pro teams in the Washington area. It was managed by Bill Jenkins, an excellent ballplayer himself.

They had come loaded for bear, to teach an old country boy a lesson for defeating them 4-3 the last time they came to town. Tick took his loss like the good sport that he was. With the Red Sox win, it made a perfect set-up for the playoff game. It was played on Labor Day.

During the '20s, 30's and 40's, baseball was the only thing for people to attend on Sundays. You could find three to four hundred or more attending a ball game on any Sunday. They completely ringed the baseball field at Leonard Hall. The large shade trees were really nice to sit under to watch the game.

The big game was set for Labor Day. The Sox, so sure they would win, brought some extra friends, rumored to be big league, ballplayers. They were prepared to feast on the good old fastballs they expected from Tick. The good old country boy, well aware of their last game and all those balls flying out of the ballpark, changed his strategy. Instead of the fastball menu, they received a mixture of changeups, curves, and that old one finger doozie ball; all this mixed with a fastball now and then to keep them off balance. When they were set for slow stuff, Tick would burn a fast one by them, and when they were set for a fast one, they received a changeup. Damn if that sly old rascal didn't hang a 2-1 defeat on them. The fans went wild. It sounded like we won the World Series. They wanted to carry Tick on their shoulders. Tick would have no part of that.

Bill Jenkins shook his head and walked away. Tick's last laugh must have been sweet, indeed. It was a big win over a semi-pro team.

Chapter Forty-Five

The Country Philosopher - Stephen Gore Uhler

Don't Listen To Your Family

The Country Philosopher
By Stephen Gore Uhler

A few of my cousins flew into town last week for the most delightful reunion. We are all about the same age and share many of the same memories of summers on grandpa's farm in Oakville and visits to the river shore at nearby Sandgates.

Quite a remarkable group, my cousins, all well-educated with successful careers in a variety of fields, so naturally they appreciate fine literature (this column, for example).

After wining, dining, and reminiscing through the evening, they began to bring up some of my old columns that they had enjoyed.

We laughed at some of the humorous columns and argued over the political ones until one of my cousins made a remark, which cut me to the core.

"Stevie, your column sometimes state facts, which are not necessarily true."

My dearest cousin, how she hurt me! I would say rather that she plunge her steak knife into my heart than to say that I had written an untruth.

Then our conversation turned to truth. What is the truth, should the truth always be told?

All of us at the table had benefited from the best ethical training at the hands of the best Jesuit Theologians. I reminded them of a question posed in class one day. "If your dear grandmother asks, "Does my new dress make me look too fat?

What do you answer? Do you tell the truth that she looks like a toothless old elephant? Of course, you don't tell the truth. Some people tell the truth all the time, just to look good.

When George Washington's father, quite angrily, asked: "who cut down his favorite cherry tree"? Little George piped right up, "I did father, I cut it down with my hatchet."

Why did George risk an ass whipping by telling the truth right away? Because he knew he wanted to be President someday. Just think how it would appear in his campaign ads, "George Washington cannot tell a lie! "That sure sounds better than "Al Gore, who cannot tell the truth."

I was hurt and offended by the subject of lies and liars. I cannot tell a lie and refuse to associate with those who do.

That being said, let me qualify it by explaining that I always tell the truth, as I perceive the truth.

I am sure all of you have seen the experiment on eyewitnesses. A group of people are shown a short film and then asked what they have seen. In the film, a brown Buick with a White top, driven by a middle-aged man with a mustache, runs through a stop sign and hits a blue Studebaker, driven by a young woman.

When the answer sheets are checked, the make and model of the automobiles are reversed, the colors change, the middle-aged man with the mustache becomes a young boy with a crew cut and the young woman in the Studebaker becomes a male oriental pulling a Rickshaw, and yet all of those subjects were trying to tell the truth.

There was a young man who used to hang around the county taverns in the years following the end of WWII, filled-up drinks with stories of his bravery. His only problem was his complete ignorance of geography. He placed himself in the middle of battles that took place on opposite ends of the Globe.

"Bastogne?" Yes, sir, that was a hellhole. I seen all of it. Wounded twice at Bastogne" "Okinawa." Man, I fought my way clear across Okinawa, medics didn't think they would be able to get me out."

And, so it went, like CBS; he was there until one of the real veterans decided to have some fun.

"Your outfit sure saw a lot of action, Leroy - How did you move around? By ship? By airplane?

"Heck, no! They marched us every step of the way."

***

Mark Twain's pet peeve was statistics. Twain said there were three kinds of lies. "Lies, damnable lies, and statistics."

Writing a column, such as this one, where truth is paramount, requires hours and hours of thorough research. There can be no mistake, no untruth. Sometimes memories are clouded by time. Sometimes you find two or more reference works. Giving opposing answers to the same question.

One can only winnow and re-winnow, keep sifting and sifting until the pure unadulterated truth comes to the surface.

I realize that we are now into the 21st century, where truth has no importance anymore, but the truth is still important to me, and you can be sure to find the true gospel under my heading.

To my cousins who insist that Mr. Dilmore couldn't have used his dead wife as crab bait, or that Leroy didn't take a tractor-trailer load of lumber down Bryantown Hill, drunk with no brakes, I can only say "You weren't there."

One form of lying that I will never be accused of is plagiarism. Of course, as every schoolboy knows, Plagiarism is the copying of another writer's work and publishing it as your own.

Shakespeare? He's dead. Twain? Dead. Hemmingway? Ditto.

There is really no author alive that I could plagiarize to improve my work.

Chapter Forty-Six

On the Trail of the Black Panther

By Cap'n Larry Jarboe

In Mid-April, I got a call to cover for a trans-Atlantic maritime lecture series from Miami to Madeira Island and Barcelona, Spain. Though the short notice to organize seven 45-minute powerpoint, presentations was an enormous challenge, the opportunity for both my wife and myself was well worth the effort.

During our presentation on the Battle of the Atlantic (1939-45), the standing-room audience who rocked gently in 15-20 foot seas was especially interested in the German stealth U-Boat that has found its final rest in 90 feet of water off Piney Point.

Did you know that a wrecked German U-Boat lays on the bottom of the Potomac River?

With the entrance of the United States into World War II after the Japanese attack on Pearl Harbor, American and British scientists and engineers began to turn the tide on the nearly invincible German U-Boat menace in the Atlantic Ocean. Coordinated improvements in ASDIC and SONAR, along with the development of forward propelled undersea hedgehog missiles coupled with depth charges from astern, made the U-Boats vulnerable to destruction from their targets above.

By the end of the war, seventy-five percent of the U-Boat crews who put to sea for the Father Land found their graves in Mother Ocean.

One of the U-Boats who escaped detection by the more sophisticated Allied SONAR was the U-1105.

On April 20, 1944, the U-1105 was launched from Emden, Germany. This was one of less than ten German submarines that had been outfitted with a rubber outer skin that absorbed SONAR pings to help avoid detection from the Allied destroyers.

Oberleutenant Hans-Joachim Schwartz was only 25 years old when he took command of this vessel.

The Germans nicknamed this U-Boat "Black Panther" due to the black rubber coating on the vessel.

On her first mission in the spring of 1945, U-1105 torpedoed and damaged the HMS Redmill, a 1300 ton frigate, which lost 32 men in the attack. When the Black Panther dove to 330 feet, she was unable to maintain depth. Instead, she lay on the bottom 570 feet down for 31 hours, evaded the Allied squadron, and escaped.

One month later, the war with Germany ended. U-1105 was surrendered to the Allies, where it was turned over to the United States for experiments and studies. Lt. Schwartz and his crew were lucky to have survived their German U-Boat duty.

The trip across the Atlantic in a hurricane had to be undertaken on the surface due to the potential of sabotaged airlines. A submarine in the depths of the ocean is one of the calmest places a seaman might be in stormy seas. A submarine on the surface of high seas is one rolling miserable place to be.

The weary American crew arrived in Portsmouth, New Hampshire, in early 1946. After research on the rubber, the skin was completed. The boat was outfitted for demolition testing by the Indian Head Naval Powder Factory. The final destruction of the sub took place in the Potomac River off Piney Point, Maryland, in 1949. There, the Black Panther lay on the bottom undetected for 36 years.

After the rediscovery of the wreck during the summer of 1985, U-1105 was archeologically surveyed from 1992-93. In November 1994, the Black Panther wreck became Maryland's first historic shipwreck preserve.

Though this is an advanced dive that I do not intend to ever attempt, there are artifacts and photographs associated with the stealth vessel in the Piney Point Lighthouse Museum that are most enjoyable to observe without ever getting wet. The volunteer staff at the museum have a passion for our local history that can only be appreciated by visiting with them.

Yes, Virginia, there is a German U-Boat lying deep off the Maryland shore.

Larry Jarboe bass21292@yahoo.com

Cap'n Larry Jarboe with his boat rigged for night fishing.

Chapter Forty-Seven

An oyster dredger at work on the Patuxent.
THE CHESAPEAKE TODAY photo

Life and Times of
Capt. Joe Lore of Solomon's Island

Part I
By Capt. J. C. Lore, Jr.

As told to Tim Flaherty

My name is Joseph Cobb Lore Jr., and I was born on Solomon's Island, Md., on the last day of the year 1900. The name Joseph C. Lore is rather well-known to locals and to long-time visitors as the Joseph C. Lore and Sons Seafood packing house operated on the Island for almost sixty years.

My father, Joseph Cobb Lore Sr., came to Calvert County in 1888 from New Jersey, where he was born in Newport, Cumberland County. He originally came here representing his uncle, who operated an oyster packing business back in New Jersey but decided to stay and open his own seafood operation.

I went to work for my father in 1920, and we first shipped oysters via parcel post to our customers in Washington, D.C., and Pennsylvania in consumer size containers. The building that is now part of the Calvert Marine Museum was built in 1934.

The first building our packing company had at that location was virtually destroyed in the Hurricane of August 1933. The building was torn to pieces, and all of the equipment was swept out onto the roadway or into the creek.

The height of the storm came on August 18[th,] and I was in Washington that morning delivering seafood. When I came to Solomon's that day, the water was up to my shoulders. Many boats had come into the creek for protection, but, of course, the storm just followed them in. The hurricane treated our oyster house in such a bad fashion that in 1934, we had the new building constructed.

Our packing company handled seafood of all kinds, mainly oysters, but also soft crabs, hard crabs, and other types indigenous to the area. I enjoyed the seafood life very much, I tell you.

My father was active in the seafood business for about seventy years. I had one brother who was also active in the business. My wife and I have two daughters, and they loved growing up around the oyster house. I would make deliveries early in the morning in Baltimore or Washington and return to Solomon's in time for lunch. When I would come out of the house to get in the car to go back to the oyster house, the kids would be hiding on the floor in the back where I couldn't see them. They'll still tell you about how much they enjoyed coming to the oyster house in this clandestine way, and about how much I chased them out. One of my sons-in-law got interested in sailing and decided to take his wife and younger son on a two-year sailboat tour of the East Coast and the Caribbean. They eventually settled in Hilton Head, South Carolina, where he became a yacht broker. His youngest son, Greg, lives in Solomon's, where he is also a yacht broker. So you see, my children and even their children share an affinity for a waterfront way of life.

Growing up, I was one of seven boys and two girls. I had three brothers in military service, and one of them was killed in World War I. Only one of my older brothers took an interest in working on the water. He went to Baltimore and became a tugboat captain. He used to come here quite often on his trips down the bay to Norfolk and other places.

Working in my father's business afforded me my first chance to visit Washington, D.C., when I was twenty-one years old. I went there with a truckload of 1,200 pounds of croakers. When I first got into town that morning, I didn't know any more than a monkey where I was. I only knew I was in Washington because I had a lot of bricks around me. My first stop ended up being at the Smithsonian. I pulled up to the front about 4 in the morning. I don't know what the people working there thought about a kid like me coming up with that truckload of fish, but they were nice and gave me directions to the fish market, and I made out fine. I met several of the wholesalers there and sold my truckload of fish to the first man I contacted. Of course, I was pleased about that.

I was fourteen the first time I ever went to Baltimore. I went there with my uncle who took me into a five and dime store. We got separated, and I became lost in the store. Of course, the store was much bigger than anything we had in Calvert, and I knew I was lost. So I went to the front door and waited until everyone left except my uncle. He had spent the entire time looking for me. That was my first experience in that big city.

Our packing house operated all year long. From fall until spring, we had oysters; in the spring of the year, fish came along. I remember that shad were very plentiful in the old days, we used to catch them right near the oyster bars in big pound nets. Later in the spring, soft crabs came along. And in later years, we turned to pick hard crabs at the packing house. We handled all kinds of seafood and enjoyed handling them.

Being in the oyster business, we usually had three "buy boats," boats that would go out and meet the oyster tongers and dredgers and buy their catch. The William B. Tennison was one of those boats. We purchased it in 1945 and considered it part of the family. Today the Tennison belongs to the Calvert Marine Museum, and you can still see it and even go for a ride on it from the Museum dock. The Tennison was our regular boat, the others operated from the Eastern Shore and would buy for us when we needed them.

We used to know everyone in the packing business up and down the Bay. So many of those people have remained our friends for years.

Of course, as a young man, my main interest was girls. I used to go to dances at Evan's Pavilion, where Solomon's Pier now stands. This was a rural community, and I guess a lot of people in the Washington and Baltimore area felt sorry for us and thought we had nothing to do, but on the contrary, we always had plenty to do. We had dances several times a year.

I didn't meet my wife at one of those dances, however. She's from Washington County, Williamsport, to be exact. I met her through a friend of mine who was a student at Western Maryland College. She used to visit here in the summer, and occasionally at

Christmas, I would visit her at her home, often, too. I might take a truckload of fish to Washington or Baltimore, come back to Solomon's, take a bath, and then jump in the car and head towards Hagerstown to see my future wife. That was quite a long trip in the 1920s, but the attraction was there. When she would visit, we would go to the dances and other functions. She enjoyed Solomon's very much and was very fascinated by it; she still is. The former Virginia Bell and I were married on August 10th, 1927.

I never seriously thought of leaving Solomon's area and taking up another line of work. Of course, it occasionally crossed my mind, but I don't think I'd find another place I'd rather be. I think that even applies to people who come here on trips, they like it so much they want to come back. Of course, long ago, everyone that wanted a job here could find one, and that helped keep people in the area. There were not only seafood operations but the shipyards like Davis Shipyards. Dr. Reginald Truitt founded the Chesapeake Bay Research Laboratory here in the '30s, so as you can tell, most everyone employed in Solomon's back then worked on or near the water.

I remember in the 1930s, there were many fishing parties that would come to Solomon's, just like today. We had a fleet of eight boats called "cruiser boats," which we would use to take parties out on fishing trips. There were a lot of boats in the community back then. Often we would take parties to the Eastern Shore and drop them off, returning to Solomon's in the pitch-black darkness.

I've done many things besides work in the seafood business that I am proud of. Recently, I went to the 50th Anniversary Dinner for the Lions Club of Calvert County. Louis Goldstein, our Maryland Comptroller, and I are the only two lifetime members of the local chapter. When we started the Lions Club here, we only had twenty-two members. Now we have over one hundred. I was raised to the degree of Master Mason in 1922 and am a life member of the Mason's Lodge. In the late '30s, I helped found the Solomon's Island Yacht Club and served as its first Commodore. In 1952, I became a charter member of Calvert County Historical Society and was its President from 1968 to 1971. The Society opened and sponsors the Calvert Marine Museum, and the results of that have been most rewarding. I am a life member of that too. There are many more organizations I have been associated with over the year, and I always liked being in service groups.

In my next column, I'll tell you about what it was like to live and work here as a boy. I'm sure it's quite different than growing up today, but I suppose many things haven't changed either.

The J. C. Lore & Sons Oyster Plant at Solomon's Island is now a part of the Calvert Marine Museum. *THE CHESAPEAKE TODAY photo*

A fishing party returning to the dock.
THE CHESAPEAKE TODAY photo

(The following story about Capt. J. C. Lore Jr.'s father was published in the Washington Times-Herald on Sept. 7, 1939.)

Times-Herald Photo

J. C. LORE, 76, 'WETS A LINE'
He found prosperity in products of the bay

J. C. Lore Sends Fleet to Gather Output of Chesapeake

By Eugene Warner
The Washington Times-Herald
SOLOMON'S ISLAND, MD. (Sept. 7, 1939) – Sometimes you have to go a long way to find out what you want to know. Look at Columbus. I had to come way down here to find out we're going to have the best oysters in 12 years this season. So, everybody in Washington, get your palates on edge for the fattest, tastiest

oysters in years. Yummy! Please pass the lemon.

J. C. Lore, 76, pipe stuck in his yellowish-gray mustache, specs on his forehead, oldest fisherman on the island – and the most prosperous – gave me the good news in his spotless, white fish and oyster packing plant hard by the Patuxent.

Tidings Confirmed

His son, G. I. Rupert Lore, who weighs close to 225 and who calls himself Dick, confirmed the tidings. Another son, Joe, was too busy getting ready for the coming season to waste time talking to a reporter.

"I been in the business all my life, and I can't figure out what makes 'em good," the old man said. "Sometimes they are, sometimes they aren't, but this year's crop, for some reason I can't explain, is a jim-dandy. Fat, clean of spawn, healthy. They're fine. Best in years."

Bobbing at the end of the dock were five new boats, ready were the tongs, which look like two long-handled garden rakes fixed together scissorwise, and all that was stopping action was the absence of an "r" in the month. That "r" business is silly, now that we have refrigeration. Oysters are as good to eat in the summer-time as clams, but the superstition prevails in Maryland. In other areas, they eat oysters the year 'round.

Crab Season Over

The crab season is just about over. All summer long, the Lores b buy crabs from boys and fishermen up and down the Ba, which is literally crawling with the pale, green little fellows. Anybody can catch enough for a meal with only a butterfly net and boat in a half hour. Every season they sell 12 to 15 thousand dozen crabs. I hope you don't have a nightmare tonight trying to visualize them.

They make a lot of money out of oysters and crabs. Free raw material. All you have to do is go out and get it. Their business in a relatively short time has grown from a little seaside operation to a business serving customers around the nation. They operate from several ports with a fleet of boats (they're all brand new cruisers, good enough to be called yachts), a fleet of trucks which deliver as far away as Madison, Wis., Detroit, Cincinnati, Cleveland, New York and Miami with Washington the principal market; the business supports three families handsomely. In the spring, the shad come. Last spring, the Lore's netted 250,264 pounds of fish and sold them. They shuck and sell 85,000 bushels of oysters a year, getting six pints to the bushel. Ice is the keynote of the business; the seafood is kept iced constantly from the river bottom to the dinner plate.

"We used to catch sturgeon around here," old J. C. recollected. "And we'd get several water buckets full of roe from each one. All I did for eleven weeks a year was pack caviar, but it doesn't do me any good, because the sturgeon are all gone. Haven't seen one in years."

His biggest thrill in 76 years of fishing was dipping a net in the Bay and hauling up ten tons of channel bass in one dip. That's a lot of bass.

Old J. C. was one of the pioneers in planting oyster shells on the shallow oyster bars. The practice is bringing back the oyster. Formerly the shells were cast aside or ground up into lime and fertilizer. But J. C. figured the baby oysters, or "spat," the larvae, so tiny they can't be seen with the naked eye, needed rough moorings to grip. So he wrote a good many letters to the late Gov. Albert C. Ritchie of Maryland trying to get the State to do something. Now the State plants 2,000,000 bushels of shells a year. The industry has benefitted.

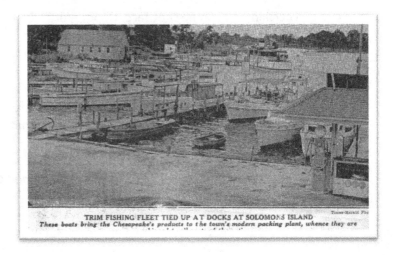

TRIM FISHING FLEET TIED UP AT DOCKS AT SOLOMONS ISLAND
These boats bring the Chesapeake's products to the town's modern packing plant, whence they are

Chapter Forty-Eight

Self Service Blues

The Country Philosopher
By Stephen Gore Uhler

Whatever became of the countermen we had back in the good old days? You know, the polite, knowledgeable persons who would listen to your vague description of some product you needed and return from the warehouse with exactly the piece you needed.

This self-service crap might work in grocery stores, but there is no substitute for good service in auto parts, hardware stores, or such.

Go into one of these modern" hardware stores and ask for help with a certain item. Some snot-face dropout, drawing the minimum wage and overpaid at that, will walk you up and down all the aisles in the emporium, "I seen it somewhere," he will whine as he exits each aisle.

Sure enough, hardware clerks like we had in the good old days would not only fetch up the part you needed but could tell you exactly how to install the item, but also how many and what size screws you'd need.

Rodney Thompson, who clerked at the old Dean Lumber before they moved out on the highway and became "Home Center," comes to mind.

Rodney could explain in precise detail how to use any of the thousands of products in the store, and yet I know Rodney never held a tool in his own hands. He must have picked up his knowledge by eavesdropping on the real mechanics who hung around the store talking shop.

Auto Parts places are a riot. They don't stock a damn thing except for a computer screen.

"I don't have it, but there's one in Billings, Montana. I could probably get it here before next Saturday."

That is just what you want to hear when your car is halfway between Oraville and Morganza with the hood up!

When I think of auto parts, I think of Ernest Wheeler. Ernest knew every auto part that had ever been machined, stamped or cast, its part number and location in the bins behind him.

You could find some worn, rusted, bent up piece of metal lying in your driveway. "What's this offa, Ernest?"

"Relax, Stephen, it's not off of your old Ford. That's a wheel cylinder spring retainer off a Chevrolet. Part number 5698-A. If it were off the left side, it would be 5698-B, fits all models '47 to '59 except the sport coupe."

Try buying an auto part today.

Some bosomy blonde with eye shadow and lip-blush who couldn't tell an alternator from a mud flap will point you to her ultra-modern, self-help computer screen, a torture device that the Torquemada would have considered too inhumane.

Make of vehicle, the machine asks.

Punch in F-O-R-D.

Car or truck?

Punch in T-R-U-C-K.

Model Year?

Punch in 1-9-8-9.

Size of engine?

Run out to the parking lot, raise the hood, wipe off the data plate with your bare hand, burning the hell out of yourself in the process, run back in and punch in 7.5 L-I-T-R-E-S.

Amperage of alternator.

Damn! Back outside, raise the hood, back inside.

Too late! Some cretin has erased your data and is punching in something about an oil filter for an '84 Toyota.

Now, I know what you are thinking. "What is Stephen Uhler doing toting his own auto parts? Surely, a man of his station in life, with his wealth, his handsome good looks, his sparkling personality, surely he doesn't have to crawl under his own vehicles with a handful of wrenches?

Why doesn't he send them out for repair?"

The last time I had my pickup in the shop was when I had a loose cover on my right front brake, nothing serious, just a rattling cover, but I decided to go ahead and do a full brake job on the front with new rotors and discs. So I left it at the shop, and the mechanic wrote up the ticket for a complete front brake overhaul.

And, by the way, I told the mechanic, check and repack the front bearings while you have them off.

The bill was over $600 for the brake job and get this, the bill for packing bearings on two wheels was $189.00.

Stiff bill, I thought, but at least I have all new brakes on the front.

After trying a few stops, I was not satisfied with my new brakes and had to pull the wheels off myself.

I discovered that the rotors were not new; in fact, they had not even been turned. I had been taken for a sucker.

The bitter irony of being suckered was exacerbated by the fact that the mechanic had presented me with a card when I left his shop, which read, "Jesus Saves."

I didn't pay much attention to the card when he presented it, but after thinking about it, anyone who has his car fixed in that shop is going to require all the attention Jesus can give them.

Cedar Point Lighthouse ravaged by storms and vandals.

Chapter Forty-Nine

Pickerel Picking 101

By Cap'n Larry Jarboe

I promised to share a technique for picking the fine y-shaped bones out of a pickerel fillet. Armed with my favorite pickerel lure, a Zoom plastic Super Salty white pearl fluke Texas-rigged on a 3/0 snelled spinner fluke hook with a 1/16 ounce bullet lead nose, I took off to a local pond to catch a couple to fry up.

This winter has not been severely cold, but it has been cold for a long time. The best catching is yet to come as the water warms. Still, the fishing was pretty enjoyable on that delightful fifty degrees sunny late March afternoon in a leaky canoe.

The first fish on was a 3 pound plus Largemouth Bass that inhaled the soft plastic lure after a few dozen casts. Eventually, you will catch a fish if you move your lure through enough water. Not long after, another bucket mouth, a feisty one-pounder, surprised me with its tenacity. Both lip-hooked fish was gently returned to bite another day.

Finally, from the aquatic vegetation just off a mudflat, I picked up my first Eastern Chain Pickerel. This was a nice size one about twenty inches long that hung the line up in the weeds. However, the canoe was easy to move and pull the freshwater barracuda from the lily pad stems.

Later, another smaller pickerel fell for the modified pearl fluke, which might be renamed the Pickerel Plucker. Two fish swimming in the bottom of the canoe (remember the adjective, leaky) were enough for a good meal, a few pictures, and the story I promised.

Pickerel fillet like any fish. I usually leave the rib cage intact and slide the main fillet off the skin with my always sharp knife. However, as good as a pickerel fillet might look, it is still full of dozens of y-shaped bones that are embedded between the lateral line and the top of the fish's back.

Instead of cutting the bones out, which is nearly impossible without great loss of meat, I choose to pan fry the fillets golden brown. House of Autry seasoning works fine.

Then, with two forks pressed back to back, you can separate the meat between the lateral line and the top of the fillet to expose those pesky bones that look like teeth of a comb exposed out of the cooked fish flesh. It is then easy to pull the bones out with your fingers to get at those nice chunks of boneless white meat.

Picking apart fried pickerel is kind of like picking crabs. Not everyone can appreciate the work involved, but the delectable taste of this freshwater predator is worth the extra effort.

Pickerel are a much better-tasting fish than Largemouth Bass. They bite year-round, and now you know how to safely bite them back.

Big catfish ready to be fileted. *Photo by Cap'n Larry Jarboe*

Chapter Fifty

Fried Hard Crabs

Letter from Point Lookout Hotel

By Alan Brylawski

The other day one of my readers (perhaps the only one – who knows?) asked if I would reprint the recipe for fried hard-shell crabs. Yes, there is such a thing. We used to serve them at the Point Lookout Hotel "Crab House and Snack Bar," which also housed the bathhouses for the Olympic-sized swimming pool. They tore down the old Hotel – I don't know the fate of the swimming pool or the crab house – but the recipes live on!

I am not sure if I ever included the recipe in my column before, so if I didn't, here it is, and if I did, here it is again.

Actually, this will be three recipes in one. If you make griddle cakes in the morning, you'd better double the recipe so you will have enough of the mix later for the crabs. Because once you taste these – I'll bet you can't just eat one stack!

The list of ingredients is as follows:

2 ½ cups of cornmeal griddle cake mixture
½ lb. or more crab cake mixture
2 or 3 large steamed hard crabs (per person)
Old Bay seasoning (to taste)
Oil for deep frying

The ingredients for the griddle cakes are:

1 cup of yellow cornmeal
1 cup of flour
1 ½ tsp salt
1 tbsp of baking powder
2 eggs well beaten
2 cups of milk

Mix the first four ingredients. Beat the eggs until they are thick (can take five to ten minutes). The more the eggs are beaten, the lighter the cakes will be. Mix the milk with the eggs. Add the dry ingredients and stir to wet. Let stand for a few minutes before dropping by the spoonful on a hot greased (lightly) skillet or grill. Turn when the cake starts to firm on the edges. Remove when golden brown.

Save the uncooked mix so you can coat the hard crabs. Don't say I didn't warn you that if you have them for breakfast, you will have to make more for the crabs. The above will serve four normal appetites (with sausage, bacon, scrapple, or ham). If, and I hope you will, put a little Old Bay seasoning in the cornmeal griddle mix. But not the ones you are going to have for breakfast.

Crab Cake Ingredients:

1 lb. Crabmeat, 1 tsp. Salt, 2 eggs, chopped onions, 1/3 to ½ cup of breadcrumbs, pepper, 1 1/3 tbsp mustard, a dash of Tabasco, 1 tbsp of mayonnaise, a dash of Worcestershire sauce.

Mix together. Makes 6 to 8 crab cakes

FRIED HARD CRABS

Remove the back shell, legs, claws, (crack the meat – they will not be used in this) lungs – known as Devil Fingers – and apron. For those who understand that the yellow and brown stuff is the fat for the crab, mix it with the crab cake mixture. For those that think there is something else repeated here – you are WRONG and are missing a taste treat. Whichever way, pack the crab cake mixture in the cavity between two crab halves, which was left after you cleaned as instructed above. Coat the now-stuffed crab with the cornmeal griddle cake mixture. Drop it into the deep fat fryer and fry it until a golden brown. You will be startled to find that you can now eat the whole thing. The shells that frustrate some people will now disappear. Enjoy!

If you don't want to go to any trouble – go to Obrekies' of Baltimore – they still serve them. I was talking to Bob Strains' lovely wife, and she said she thought I was the first person to feed Bob a soft crab sandwich. Bob, old boy, I don't know who it was that fixed that crab for you, but it wasn't me. Having lived in Southern Maryland since 1921 and crabbed professionally as early as 1935, I know how to clean and cook a soft crab. For those that don't know here is the way:

Fried Soft Crab

Start with ONLY a live soft crab, and the softer, the better. Take a sharp knife and cut a small semi-circle just behind the eyes. This not only removes the aforesaid eyes but also puts the crab out of its misery – so to speak. Now lift, but do not remove, one corner of the back shell and with the knife remove the Devil Fingers (lungs). With the sharp point of the knife, puncture the claws (this will reduce splattering during cooking). Now you may or may not dust with seasoned flour and sauté in butter or deep fry. Normally served on a roll with tartar sauce on the side. Fantastic.

Those of you from areas without direct access to crab-bearing waters may never have eaten a soft crab sandwich or a platter of fried soft crabs. If not, try one. They can be broiled as well.

Screw up your courage and try one. If the look bothers you, close your eyes.

I was in the old Roost in Lexington Park, Md., when three gentlemen sitting next to the table where my wife Jean and I were eating, ordered lunch during what was a business conference. Two of the men ordered soft-shell crab sandwiches, and the third man seemed to have his mind more on the business at hand rather than the menu and told the waitress that he would have "the same."

When their order came, the three were still deeply engrossed in their conversation as none paid any attention to the plates in front of them. (In case you are beginning to think I am a bit nosy, the tables were very close together – and I am nosy). One of the three started to eat, then the next and finally the third and last to order stopped talking and took his first look at his lunch. Now for those who have never seen a soft crab served on a roll, let me try to describe what he saw and what he thought he saw. If the crab is of any size, and local seafood places in the Chesapeake region all generally serve nice size soft crabs, the crab will extend past and out from under the top of the roll. Its legs will curl out and under the roll as if the crab were holding on for dear life. In other words, what that gentleman saw was a gigantic spider partially covered by the top of the roll sitting on his plate. He quickly averted his eyes and looked around the room. He paled! He looked at each of his companions, who were devouring their sandwiches. Having satisfied himself that nobody was watching, he gave what could only be described as a look of loathing as he slowly pushed his plate to the center of the table where it remained until it was removed upon departure.

Speaking of being uneducated concerning crabs, I recall one day I was with an old fishing buddy, Jim Kapp. Now Jim shares my kind of humor – just a tad weird and a little cruel. This day we were standing on the dock of Oakwood Lodge jutting out into the Potomac River near Piney Point. Two fellows rowed up to us, and they were shirtless in the hot sun. It was one of those roasting days of July with no breeze, and both of them were turning a glowing red. One of them hailed us.

"Either of you fellas know anything about crabs?"

"Yep," said Jim.

"How come these crabs we caught are green?"

"What side of Piney Point did you catch 'em on?"

We could see that they had about three-quarters of a bushel of hard crabs that they must have dipped while just polling the flats.

"This side," said one of the men.

"WELL, NO WONDER," hollered Jim. "The ripe ones are on the other side of Piney Point."

Before I could stop them, they dumped their near full basket of crabs overboard and hollered back to us, "thanks" as they were rowing away.

I remember telling Jim that we better get the heck out of there before they wake up and come back. I can only hope that whoever they were, that they don't read this and come back for revenge.

Chapter Fifty-One

Follow the Dolphin

By Vi Englund

Does the sea beckon you? Do tall ships sail sleepless nights? Do you feel the lure of the Dolphin? Sometimes do you just want to chuck it all and go? Yet when you start to make your move, does your apprehension seek a loophole? Trembling, do you slide through it into the comfortable arms of your easy chair? You nestle there feeling you are a pluckless wonder – secure in the comfort you have structured. Friend! I've been there. You may be on a collision course with a sea myth. I won many a battle with mine, but I lost the war.

Now, I know why I fought so hard. Comfort is mighty cozy, and it's rough out there. My dream ships never ripped a sail in a gale. I never saw a rusty chain plate, a snapped turnbuckle, a dragging anchor, a frayed halyard, a leaky bilge, or a snarled line on a cloud ship. A ship in the sky is not like a ship afloat. And a man and woman living together on a boat is a proving ground for survival.

I learned fooling around with boats is like starting a new romance. Sometimes you get somewhere you didn't know you were going.

We'd migrated to the Virgin Islands. He served as master of a 73' schooner, *Tontine II.* A lovely lady laced with varnish and teak and mystique of the sea in every line.

I sensibly worked ashore as a travel agent.

On the day before a charter, his cook quit.

"Guess what?" he said.

"Not me," I said. "I can cook but not out at sea."

"No different," he said. He studied the tip of the golden mast with his honest blue eyes. Glibly, he added. "You're just a natural-born sea woman."

I beamed. "You really think so?"

At this moment, I lost the war.

I sailed through the first charter season on his trust, my enthusiasm, and the capacity to work endowed to me from my pioneer stock.

In April, he set the course for New England.

As I ricocheted around the galley cooking for a seven-man crew, I felt a seasoned salt. But after Bermuda, the salt lost some of its savor.

I stood braced in the corner of the galley with my feet planted, body alist, peeling a stew onion. The spoon bow of Tontine II slammed as if she struck a rock. The boat shuddered. Yet we were five hundred miles north of Bermuda in water five miles deep. At the hatch, I watched a wave lift and could almost smell its power. It lifted high, higher – until it reached the spreader on the foremast. The indigo seas left deep caverns. The shrouds transformed the wind's moan to a shriek. The wave slammed the deck. I sucked in my breath as though struck by a jibing boom. Disbelief – sheer disbelief froze every nerve. This was no ocean I knew.

I recalled an old saying.

"A man who would go to sea for pleasure should go to hell for a pastime."

The Captain yelled, "We've got to lay to."

A sea whelmed us, the vessel lurched, and I lay flat on my back on the galley deck. I contemplated the overhead and thought, And Old Long John Silver Tongue said it was no different to cook at sea.

Yet as the hydraulic force pounded the vessel, I had my first primitive lesson in boat design and construction. I listened to the beams groan and felt the stirring of profound respect. The Captain laid to, she eased off. I felt the relationship between the man and his boat, and the boat and the sea. A combination honed by centuries of seamanship, they conform to the sea's demand.

We arrived in Wickford, Rhode Island, five days late with a sound vessel and elated crew. Gaining a foothold on the dock with motion-weak knees, I felt nothing on land could ever intimidate me again.

The Skipper, his face seamed by weather, his eyes tired, coiled a line. *Tontine II* lay mute and sea shabby. Tears formed as I fell in love with a collection of salt-stained teak shaped like a schooner.

At sea, a man meets himself head-on. If he survives the shock, he may find something that keeps him going back, in spite of that discovery – and he finds contentment in doing that.

You'll never know what's out there for you until you go and find out.

Chapter Fifty-Two

PRESIDENT BUSH SENDS CARRIER ATTACK GROUP TO HUNT U-BOAT IN CHESAPEAKE

Vows to protect shipping

(SPECIAL) SOLOMON'S ISLAND, MD. --- A complete U. S. Navy Task Force arrived in the Chesapeake Bay on July 8th to set the final net for entrapping the marauding German U-Boat, the Sea Dagger, that has been terrorizing the Chesapeake for the last four months. The USS Dwight Eisenhower, named after the late President who served two terms in the 1950's and as Supreme Allied Commander in Europe during WWII is an ironic choice to lead the U. S. Naval forces assigned to ferreting out an ancient U-Boat that has been frustrating Naval forces and the Maryland Natural Resources Police for much of this year.

Not since the German submarine, U-69 entered the Chesapeake Bay and laid mines in 1942 to damage shipping transiting the Bay to and from Baltimore, has the sense of impending danger been so strong.

The carrier attack group consists of a heavy cruiser equipped with Aegis missiles, six destroyers, and two nuclear subs along with the Eisenhower.

The U-Boat, which has been causing panic on the Chesapeake in recent months, was the topic of questions to the President's press secretary at the White House just before press time:

"President George H. W. Bush has determined that that the German Captain has ignored pleas to surrender his men and his vessel and to listen to pleas from both the West German government as well as the East German officials who told the errant Nazi officer that the war has been over for decades."

"Therefore, in the interest of public safety of both pleasure craft and commercial shipping transiting the Chesapeake, I have ordered the Eisenhower Task Force to be deployed to find and, if needed, destroy the U-boat."

Some have speculated that the President's actions could be interpreted as an act of war on the German government, even though the Germans surrendered decades ago.

Historians are in complete disagreement with that view and reaction from American University President Richard Cort insisted the U-Boat, time warp or not, is the property of the Allied Forces and the U.S. is well within its rights as an Allied nation to take action against after belligerent military unit under the Geneva Accords of 1946.

Some pundits have quipped that with all the U. S. military resources devoted to tracking down the U-Boat, Navy is more likely to catch itself than the mysterious U-Boat. There has been mounting pressure on the federal government by Maryland officials to stop denying the U-Boat exists, but with this latest deployment of major naval assets to hunt down the terror from WWII ought to quell those voices.

The director of the Smithsonian Institute Center for Study of Phenomena, Dr. Donald Bucy, issued a statement saying it was patently absurd for the President to send a carrier task force to find a vessel that exists purely in the imaginations of a few people. Bucy said his scientists had been in touch with the apparitions on the U-Boat.

"We have started to make some progress in convincing the U-Boat Captain that the war is over and to transponder him back to his own time. We are starting to make some headway in convincing the U-Boat Captain that he really is in a time-warp and must stop the hostilities. With a little more time, we believe we can convince him that the war is over.

Naval historians have noted that the German sub known as Sea Dagger had a distinguished record in WWII and that it could be dangerous to send it back to 1944. One expert said that doing so could actually send more Allied shipping to the bottom of the sea because of what we do in 1989.

As the debate rages, American forces have already started to comb the Bay for this most unusual prey, the first time since WWII that U. S. Navy ships have prowled the Bay looking for enemy ships.

Tourists have been pouring into waterside towns and boosting business in Cambridge, Solomon's Island, Crisfield, Annapolis, Chesapeake Beach, and Tilghman Island, hoping to get a glimpse of the U-Boat and American ships trying to blow it out of the water.

An NBC news crew on a charter boat and another boat carrying a Phil Donohue Show crew collided in Back Creek at Solomon's Island with one boat sunk and all aboard both vessels uninjured. Natural Resources Police reported that the wreck was the sixteenth collision involving news media boats. The various media crews are out to top each other by obtaining the first interview with the U-Boat captain and crew. A mini-sub used by ABC News was hit by a

Danish news boat by Buoy 52 in the Bay and was almost run over by a Brazilian container ship. The next report will provide further details on the largest Naval force in the Chesapeake since the British Fleet invaded in 1814 and burned Washington principal government buildings prior to bombarding Fort McHenry. The Chesapeake Flotilla of the U.S. Navy battled the Royal Navy but were severely outmatched.

Chapter Fifty-Three

Pepper Langley stands in front of the street sign at Solomon's Island of the road named for his family. *Photo by Ken Rossignol*

Eel trapping days on the Patuxent

By Pepper Langley

In a prior chapter, I told you about how we caught soft crabs and sold them to the packing house in Solomon's, but I did not mention how the trotline crabbers caught their crabs. These were large hard crabs caught on a line about a ½ mile long. These lines had a buoy and an anchor on each end, which was baited with eel bait, about every three feet apart.

Then the crabber would run his crab boat down this line with the crab bait coming up over the roller, which was mounted on the side of the boat. When the line came up and had a crab on it, the crabber would dip it with a wire crab net. The crab would be tossed in a crab barrel.

Before the crabber could catch his crabs, he had to get that eel bait on the line. He couldn't crab and catch eels both, so he had to have someone catch his eels. That was my job. I worked to catch eels for the crabbers.

At the age of fifteen, I began trapping eels. Our eel traps were 10 inches in diameter and three feet long with three iron rings fastening them, one on each end and one in the center of the trap. Each one of these rings was wired inside of the wire net, which was a 3/8-inch mesh galvanized wire. Each ring had a trap load to the rings; on one end was the net where the eels went in; the next was the net in the middle where the eels also had to get through to the crab bait. The crab bait was in the last section, and the last ring had a net with the drawstring that we would untie to take the eels out.

Where we set our nets was on a section of the river that we had put the crab pickings that come from the crab packing house that was discarded. There was no better place to put these remains of the crab picking process than back in the water where the eels could eat them. What that eel didn't know was while he was eating the crab pickings, the next day, a crab would be eating him. That was the life cycle of crabs and eels.

At that time, I was setting fifty eel traps a day, and I would be towed out to the eel set area by the crabber at four in the morning. As soon as I could see the corks floating on the water that was attached to our eel trap, I would pick them up, and when I got them all, I would take them ashore to process the traps.

I would remove the eels from the traps and put them in a barrel that the crabber had set up with a lime solution in it that would kill the eels and remove the slime off them.

When the crabber came home from crabbing, he would get his lunch go back down to the shore from his home to the little boathouse. Then he would gut the eels and take off the heads. He then put the eels in a salt solution in another barrel until the next day. After spending the night in the salt barrel, the eels were removed and packed in dry salt. What he did not use for bait were then shipped to Baltimore, where they were smoked and sold for those who enjoyed eating eels.

If you have never tasted eel, you should try it. I used to throw out two or three of the biggest eels and set them aside to take home. I would cut them into 3-inch sections and fry them in real butter, and they were great eating. Add a little lemon too, and they are really a better meal than most saltwater fish. The taste is much like sea trout. When you are fixing your own fresh eel, please think of me as it's been a long time since I have seen one big enough to eat. – Have a good eel-trapping day!

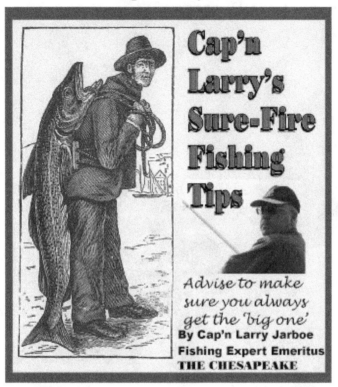

Chapter Fifty-Four

Cap'n
Larry's
Sure-Fire
Fishing
Tips

*Advise to make
sure you always
get the 'big one'*
By Cap'n Larry Jarboe
Fishing Expert Emeritus
THE CHESAPEAKE

Year-Round Fishing on the Patuxent River

By Cap'n Larry Jarboe

On the Western Shore of the Chesapeake Bay, the Patuxent River begins in Maryland and ends in Maryland's Bay waters. This historic river whose shores were home to many generations of native Eastern American Indian tribes is still a place of both waterfront residential properties and recreational opportunities.

The lower Southern Maryland portion of the Patuxent River is bounded by St. Mary's, Calvert, Charles, and Prince Georges Counties. In addition to the historic and scenic value this river offers, there are very unique environmental characteristics, both natural and manmade, that make the Patuxent a prime place to fish during any season of the year.

Believe it or not, you can start your New Year off as well as any East Coast angler can by fishing relatively warm and always calm waters of the Chalk Point power plant discharge canal. The power plant can be easily accessed by launching at the Department of Natural Resources public boat ramp at Barstow on Route 231 in Calvert County.

A three-mile run up the river past the large power plant will bring you to the narrow mouth of the warm water discharge canal, which is just downstream of the riverside community of Eagle Harbor in Prince Georges County.

The water depth runs over ten-foot deep through most of the manmade canal, which winds back to the power plant where the towers are cooled. A floating scum barrier blocks close access to the facility, but a variety of fish may be caught in the half-mile space between the mouth of the canal and the barrier.

Probably, the most important factor in fishing the flat calm waters of this canal in January, February, or early March is to have proper life jackets, better yet, a life raft as well. Also, mount an auxiliary motor on your boat's stern if you do not have twin engines to get you back home should you encounter mechanical problems. Likely, there will be no one else on the river at that time of year to provide immediate assistance.

Channel, White, and Blue Catfish are the usual quarry this time of year. Fresh peeled shrimp on standard double hook bottom rigs is the most available bait. However, cut Mud Shad is also a good bet if you have a source or are lucky enough to snag one though specifically trying to snag a Mud Shad is illegal in Maryland. Soft-shell clam snouts are also another excellent bait during cold weather. A local fish house is probably the best place to find good bait this time of year.

The most important time to fish in the Chalk Point discharge canal is from one hour after high tide to one hour before low tide. The outgoing tide pushes food, warm water, and fish down the canal past the scum barrier to the few hardy fishermen who wait for a bite in cold weather. Though the water has been warmed by the cooling towers, the water temperature in January or February might be only in the mid-forty degree range.

The colder the weather, the closer I usually fish to the plant. All the way through the creek, you will mark fish on your fish recorder. Most of these are Mud Shad, who hole up in the canal, but I believe the bigger fish close to the bottom are catfish. Channel Cats from 2 to 12 pounds are common, but the Blue Cats are taking over the ecosystem. In a few years, twenty pound Blue Cats should be a staple winter time catch in this canal. The native White Cats are not nearly so big. If you catch a seven-pound White Catfish, register it for the Maryland record.

Two years ago, I fished the discharge canal on New Year's Day and caught a nice mess of Channel Cats, which became not only woodstove cooked dinners but the first fish pics of the year for 2011 at the Tackle Box bait and supply shop in Lexington Park.

This year, Mike Henderson, Tommy Donaldson, and I fished the canal in mid-February. We caught and released a couple dozen small Red Drum that were wintering in the canal. Also, we had a cooler full of Channel cats and small tasty Blue Cats for the dinner table. You may also catch White Perch with beetle spins cast alongside the shore grass and an occasional Striped Bass or Largemouth Bass. However, you can count on catching those catfish while most fishermen are home longing for the weather to warm up.

From mid-February to mid-March, Yellow Perch can be caught by dedicated fishermen who figure when the Yellow Neds are making their spawning run. Usually, the last week of February or the first week of March is a good time to anchor at the lower fork of the Western Branch of the Patuxent to dunk Bull Minnows or Grass Shrimp in pursuit of those elusive but beautiful yellow and black striped fish.

The easiest public ramp to launch your boat to reach the Western Branch is the Jug Bay Natural Area Park that is on Croom Airport Road in Prince Georges County. The boat ramp in this park is a couple miles below where the Patuxent River forks and Yellow Perch school up in deeper water before making their annual spawning run to shallow gravel creek beds.

Though the White Perch start moving upriver in April and May, they can be finicky. By this time, the catfish are roaming throughout the mid and upper Patuxent River. Look for holes or obstructions on the bottom and fish a moving tide, either outgoing or incoming. Put out larger baits for the catfish and fish smaller hooks for the White Perch. Upriver, Tidal Largemouth Bass wait to nail soft plastic baits flipped into shore cover.

June is when a variety of fish arrive from their migration from the Atlantic Ocean up the Chesapeake Bay into the Pax River. Also, the large female Grass Shrimp start releasing their eggs in the grass along the creeks. These little shrimp are an excellent bait that is easy to catch for anyone willing to invest in a fine mesh shrimp net and a pair of rubber boots to walk the shoreline.

The many oyster bars in the Patuxent River are a good place to hunt for Atlantic Croaker, White Perch, Norfolk Spot, and Striped Bass from early summer to fall. Armed with a pound of fresh shrimp, a mess of live Grass Shrimp, and a dozen bloodworms, you are ready to catch a cooler full of good eating panfish from the edge of the oyster bars.

The trick to fishing those living reefs is to anchor up tide on the top of the oyster bar (maybe 8'-11' of water) and feed out anchor line till you drop off the edge of the bar and lay in about 15 feet of water. The moving tide will push food quickly across the top of the bar. Larger croakers, perch, and rockfish will lie in wait below the top of the bar in slower water to grab bait that is pushed over the edge. Double hook bottom rigs with a one-ounce bell sinker are the ticket here. Small live spot hooked through the back on a live bait rig will also help put your limit of two Striped Bass in the boat.

In July and August, the warmer weather really heats up the action on those oyster bars as the migratory species compete with the native fish for food. By this time, peeler crabs and soft crabs become available for bait and should be added to the arsenal as the larger Grass Shrimp have spawned out and mostly smaller harder to hook ones become most common in the push net. Also, cut spot is also a good bait that you can likely catch and recycle for Striped Bass, White Perch, and all types of catfish.

Summertime is when the creeks become good places to catch lots of fish if you can locate holes, underwater obstructions, or the mouth of feeder creeks. Bottom rigs or beetle spins pulling white, or chartreuse 1 1/2" Mister Twisters will catch a wide variety of fish on either moving tide.

By this time, most fishermen will focus on fishing early morning or late evening to avoid the heat. The challenge is to coordinate your time to fish with the moving tide. The Maryland Department of Natural Resources has an excellent tide table on their website. Prior to any fishing trip, you should consult both the weather forecast and the tide tables for the day you intend to fish.

September is my favorite time of the year for both fishing and catching in the Patuxent River. A smorgasbord of fish species will be taking advantage of the generally mild weather and moderate temperatures in Maryland to fatten up for the winter chill ahead.

You can fish pretty much anytime during the day as long as the tide is moving. Though night fishing is good throughout the summer, my best Patuxent evening catches have come in September before the first frost. I remember one evening September trip that we caught a huge mess of Striped Bass, White Perch, Atlantic Croaker, Norfolk Spot, Red Drum, Weakfish, Channel Catfish, White Catfish, Bluefish, Toadfish, Blue Crabs, and a monster American Eel that was slung into the boat after the sun had set. That eel made a huge mess in the boat all by itself.

This great variety of fish came from the edge of the ledge of Buzzard Island oyster bar, where the water drops from 10' of depth to over 40' on the Eastern side of the channel. This hot spot is direct across from Golden Beach only about a mile below the DNR ramp at Barstow. Though there are many public and private ramps on both sides of the Patuxent, the Barstow ramp is most convenient to all the Southern Maryland counties.

In October, the trollers will find Striped Bass stacked up from Buzzard Island Bar south to Sheridan Point. Small to medium bucktails dragged slowly above the bottom from daybreak to mid-morning should get your limit of these rockfish that school up in the deeper mid-river channel to feed before moving into the Chesapeake Bay.

When the waters chill in November and December, some Striped Bass may be found in the mouth of the Patuxent. White Perch can be caught jigging in the hundred-foot depths under the Solomon's Bridge on Route 4. Or, you can enjoy catching fish in a barrel that has taken refuge in the warmer water of the Chalk Point Power Plant discharge canal. You never know what creature might find respite from the cold in these warm waters. A few years ago, a manatee surfaced beside my 20' Shamrock boat while I was catching Channel Catfish in the discharge canal in mid-November.

No, manatees are not to be expected fishing partners in the Patuxent River, but occasional renegades make their way up the East Coast. That particular marine mammal did not stay in the manmade power plant hot tub for the winter. His carcass was retrieved from the shore of the Patuxent, and his bones reside downriver at the Calvert Marine Museum in Solomon's, Maryland.

Unlike that manatee who ventured into the Patuxent River and stayed too long, your luck will be likely far better if you follow a few simple fishing tricks:

Remember to check the weather forecast and the tide tables for the area you intend to fish. Make sure your boat is well maintained with proper safety equipment and an auxiliary motor to get home. Find good fresh bait and place it where resident and migratory fish are likely to bite upon it.

Where else in the Chesapeake region can you enjoy both fishing for and catching fish year-round within a few miles from a public boat ramp? The Patuxent River is one of the best-kept secrets in the State of Maryland.

Let's keep it to ourselves.

Larry Jarboe - bass21292@yahoo.com

Captain Larry Jarboe now operates Eco-tours of the Everglades at Key Largo, Florida.

Chapter Fifty-Five

The Historic Chesapeake Bay Oyster Buyboats

By Ken Rossignol

Visiting each year at various locations around the Chesapeake is a collection of historic Chesapeake Bay Oyster Buyboats. They often assemble at Fitzie's Marina on Breton Bay, and some can be seen at the annual Blessing of the Fleet, sponsored by the 7th District Optimist Club.

The wheelhouse of the F. D. Crockett shows the painstaking care which has been provided by the teams of volunteers at the Deltaville Maritime Museum to bring the historic oyster Buyboat back to life. John England said that the ship was headed towards the boat graveyard, as shown below on Nomini Bay, when the volunteers decided to tackle the task.

THE CHESAPEAKE TODAY photo.

The present owner and master of the Iva W., Scott, hosts a family for a tour of the pilothouse and even the engine room of the ship. The Iva W has had three engines in its lifetime, with the Caterpillar 13000 diesel engine, which was installed about the end of WWII.

What may be the world's largest assembly of Oyster Buyboats.
THE CHESAPEAKE TODAY photo

THE CHESAPEAKE TODAY photo

Johnny Ward of Deltaville was but 26 years old when the Iva W was launched
for him to captain. The vessel hauled all manner of freight, including
watermelons, lumber, oysters, crabs, tomatoes, and cabbage and in later
years, seed oysters. The ship has been remodeled and restored with the
pilothouse elevated to provide a cabin. The Iva W owner delights crowds
around the bay with visits and tours and invites folks to invite him to visit
their ports and events. THE CHESAPEAKE TODAY photo

Dave Wright, the owner of the Prop Wash, displays prior names of the
historic oyster Buyboat next to the pilothouse of the vessel.
THE CHESAPEAKE TODAY photo

This view of the hold of the F. D. Crockett shows how the bottom of the ship
was built from logs. This hold was part of the storage area for oysters as they
were also carried on the deck. The oyster buyboats were an important link
from those who tonged the oysters to the surface and sold them to the

Captain of the Buyboat, who then transported them to wharves in Norfolk, Baltimore, Crisfield, Alexandria and Washington, D.C.
THE CHESAPEAKE TODAY photo

After a hard day sailing up the Potomac, these captains prepare for explaining to visitors what a buyboat is and how they functioned. John England, at right, led the effort to save the F.D. Crockett, the oldest logboat in Virginia. THE CHESAPEAKE TODAY photo

IVA W underway.

This historic Oyster Buyboat, the F.D. Crockett, was almost a total loss and beyond saving except for its historical significance, according to the man who led the effort to restore it. John England and the many volunteers of the Deltaville Maritime Museum performed thousands of hours of labor and raised the money needed for materials.
THE CHESAPEAKE TODAY photo

A stern day on Breton Bay as the world's largest flotilla of Chesapeake Bay Oyster Buyboats assembles for free public tours guided by those who have lovingly preserved these famous vessels. THE CHESAPEAKE TODAY photo

Buyboats on Breton Bay, Poppa Francis from Iva W

The bow of a historic Buyboat as it enters Cape Charles, Va., harbor.
THE CHESAPEAKE TODAY photo

Iva W built in 1929 is one of only a few two-deck oyster buyboats.
THE CHESAPEAKE TODAY photo

Historic Buyboats arrive at Breton Bay off of the Potomac River.
THE CHESAPEAKE TODAY photo

The Poppa Francis on display at Breton Bay.
THE CHESAPEAKE TODAY photo

Buyboat's last days in the final resting place on Nomini River, Virginia.
THE CHESAPEAKE TODAY photo

The rust streaks on the hull of the P. E. Pruit are a hint of the yearly maintenance that the owners must provide out of their pockets to preserve this part of American history. **THE CHESAPEAKE TODAY photo**

Samuel M Bailey on Potomac. THE CHESAPEAKE TODAY photo

Sam Bailey, the grandson of the man for whom the Samuel M. Bailey was named, visited the assembly of famous Chesapeake Bay Oyster Buyboats. Bailey noted that his brother's boat, the Samuel M. Bailey, is the youngest of those buyboats in the flotilla. It was built in 1957.

THE CHESAPEAKE TODAY photo

The busy harbor of Leonardtown with the invasion of the Buyboats.

Dave Wright, the owner of the "Prop Wash," participates in an annual tour of the Chesapeake region, which allows visitors to visit the buyboats. THE CHESAPEAKE TODAY photo

The Prop Wash rides at anchor in the Potomac for the annual Blessing of the Fleet. *THE CHESAPEAKE TODAY photo*

Prop Wash is a meticulously restored Buyboat. *THE CHESAPEAKE TODAY*

Dave Wright recounts the history of the Prop Wash.
THE CHESAPEAKE TODAY

IVA W is a rare two-deck Buyboat from its service as a bed and breakfast vessel. *THE CHESAPEAKE TODAY photo*

The wheelhouse.

Poppa Francis still works the Bay planting oyster seeds and is shown here in the distance. *THE CHESAPEAKE TODAY photo*

Motoring from Breton Bay into the Potomac for their next visit to a Chesapeake area port, the floating museum heads to Washington, D.C. THE CHESAPEAKE TODAY photo

A popular vessel on the tourist circuit around the Chesapeake is the R. E. Pruitt. *THE CHESAPEAKE TODAY*

Capable of traveling the east coast, the IVA W is comfortably appointed, and the owner guides tours through the vessel.

The top deck affords the Captain an unlimited view of the waters as the IVA W cruises. *THE CHESAPEAKE TODAY photos*

Nellie Crockett shows off great lines.

Imagine that! A visitor gets the feel of the wheel in the bridge of the IVA W.
THE CHESAPEAKE TODAY photo

A great visit for kids. The boat owners greet visitors for free tours as they explain the history of the historic Buyboats.

Well maintained in every way, the owners of the Buyboats care for every detail.

Uncomplicated and efficient helm of the Prop Wash.

Prior names of the vessel are listed.

This Buyboat served the oyster fleet on Wicomico River near Rock Point in Charles County, Maryland, in this 1930's photo taken by the WPA.

BE SURE TO GET ANOTHER BOOK FREE!

www.ThePrivateerClause.com

Additional books available in Kindle, paperback and Audible at Amazon and retailers worldwide

MURDER USA: True Crime, Real Killers

The Marsha & Danny Jones Thrillers

1 The Privateer Clause
#2 Return of the Sea Empress
#3 Follow Titanic
#4 Follow Triangle – Vanish!
#5 Cruise Killer
#6 BEHEADED- Terror by Land, Sea & Air
#7 Who Collects the Souls
#8 Panama Gold

SIX KILLER THRILLER NOVELS - Marsha & Danny Jones Thriller
Series Books 1 – 6

Additional books by Ken Rossignol
Chesapeake 1850
Chesapeake 1880
Chesapeake 1910

Battle of Solomon's Island

Titanic Series
Titanic 1912
Titanic & Lusitania- Survivor Stories (with Bruce M. Caplan)
Titanic Poetry, Music & Stories

The Chesapeake Series
The Chesapeake: Tales & Scales (with Larry Jarboe)
The Chesapeake: Legends, Yarns & Barnacles (with Larry Jarboe)
The Chesapeake: Oyster Buyboats, Ships & Steamed Crabs
The Chesapeake: A Man Born To Hang Can Never Drown
The Chesapeake: Country Cornpone Cornucopia
The Chesapeake: Tidewater Sagas

Non-fiction
KLAN: Killing America
Panama 1914
The Story of The Rag
Leopold & Loeb Killed Bobby Franks (with Bruce M. Caplan)
Bank of Crooks & Criminals

CHESAPEAKE CRIME CONFIDENTIAL
Coke Air: Chesapeake Crime Confidential

PIRACY and PIRATES – Non-fiction
Pirate Trials: Dastardly Deeds & Last Words

Pirate Trials: Hung by the Neck Until Dead
Pirate Trials: Famous Murderous Pirate Book Series
Pirate Trials: The Three Pirates – Islet of the Virgin

Four Pirate Novels of Murder, Executions, Romance & Treasure - **Pirate Trials Series Books 1 – 4**

Fire Cruise
Cruising the Waterfront Restaurants of the Potomac

The Traveling Cheapskate series:
The Ninety-Nine Cent Tour of Bar Harbor Maine
Boating Chesapeake Bay

CPSIA information can be obtained
at www.ICGtesting.com
Printed in the USA
LVHW091327030121
675560LV00009B/1638